2016

Guideposts
DAILY PLANNER

Guideposts

New York

Thou shalt have no other gods before me. —EXODUS 20:3 (KJV)

A PRAYER FOR JANUARY

God be in my head
and in my understanding;
God be in my eyes
and in my looking;
God be in my mouth
and in my speaking;
God be in my heart
and in my thinking;
God be at my end
and at my departing.

AUTHOR UNKNOWN (CIRCA 1514)

THE FIRST COMMANDMENT

Almighty God,
In my mind's eye I see
Your hard and fast commandments
as a mighty arch
spanning a firmament.
It is a marvel of masonry,
this arch: ten stones,
ingeniously placed
So that the strength of each
communicates to all.
And there, in the center,
topmost,
lies the keystone
Without which all the rest
would
tumble
into
chaos.
That central stone?
The unmistakable decree
That You take precedence with me.

Almighty God,
Architect of life,
Deep in my heart
I see Your clear commandments
As a master plan for me,
With You the center,
The solid keystone of my years.

❧ JANUARY 2016 ❧

SUNDAY	MONDAY	TUESDAY	WEDNESDAY	THURSDAY	FRIDAY	SATURDAY
					1 NEW YEAR'S DAY	2
3	4	5	6	7	8	9
10	11	12	13	14	15	16
17	18 MARTIN LUTHER KING JR. DAY	19	20	21	22	23 *grandma B day*
24 31	25	26	27	28	29	30

NOTES

DECEMBER 2015

S	M	T	W	T	F	S
		1	2	3	4	5
6	7	8	9	10	11	12
13	14	15	16	17	18	19
20	21	22	23	24	25	26
27	28	29	30	31		

FEBRUARY

S	M	T	W	T	F	S
	1	2	3	4	5	6
7	8	9	10	11	12	13
14	15	16	17	18	19	20
21	22	23	24	25	26	27
28	29					

OUR PRAYER

*Lord, reveal Yourself to me this year
through the good and the bad. Amen.*

DECEMBER 2015 **27** SUNDAY	A time to keep and a time to throw away. —Ecclesiastes 3:6 (NIV)
28 MONDAY	Therefore, as God's chosen people, holy and dearly loved, clothe yourself with compassion, kindness, humility, gentleness and patience. —Colossians 3:12 (NIV)
29 TUESDAY	"Do thyself no harm. . . ." —Acts 16:28 (KJV)

WHEN I WAS A BOY growing up in the Philippine Islands, New Year's Eve was always a time of intense celebration. My friends and I would buy bags full of firecrackers and skyrockets and spend the night in deafening explosive delight. My mother always worried that I would blow off my fingers; my dad just sat back and chuckled, wishing he were a boy again.

Now my New Year's Eve is a quiet time for meditation and contemplation. I love to build a big fire in the fireplace, feel its warmth, and stare into the flames and embers. With a cup of coffee in hand, I reflect on the events of the past year in the world, in our country, and in my own life. Slowly, a sense of gratitude wells up within me as I realize that God has guided me through another year. And as I face the future, I'm reminded that whatever happens, God, my Good Shepherd, will be walking with me.

30
WEDNESDAY

Tribulation worketh patience; and patience, experience; and experience, hope.
—Romans 5:3–4 (KJV)

31
THURSDAY

NEW YEAR'S EVE

A heart at peace gives life to the body. . . . —Proverbs 14:30 (NIV)

JANUARY

1
FRIDAY

NEW YEAR'S DAY

But when he, the Spirit of truth, comes, he will guide you into all the truth. He will not speak on his own; he will speak only what he hears, and he will tell you what is yet to come. —John 16:13 (NIV)

2
SATURDAY

For God, who gives seed to the farmer to plant, and later on, good crops to harvest and eat, will give you more and more seed to plant and will make it grow so that you can give away more and more fruit from your harvest. —2 Corinthians 9:10 (TLB)

Joseph Gilmore's words, written more than a century ago, are words of faith and hope for all of us: "Whate'er I do, where'er I be, still 'tis God's hand that leadeth me!"

—*Scott Walker*

PRAYER REQUESTS _____

_____

_____

_____

JANUARY

S	M	T	W	T	F	S
					1	2
3	4	5	6	7	8	9
10	11	12	13	14	15	16
17	18	19	20	21	22	23
24/31	25	26	27	28	29	30

OUR PRAYER

Lord, let me never forsake the responsibilities and blessings in front of me for the sake of what You've not yet given.

3
SUNDAY

Then Jesus spoke to them again, saying, "I am the light of the world. He who follows Me shall not walk in darkness, but have the light of life." —John 8:12 (NKJV)

4
MONDAY

And on the seventh day God finished the work that he had done, and he rested on the seventh day from all the work that he had done. —Genesis 2:2 (NRSV)

5
TUESDAY

O sing to the Lord a new song; sing to the Lord, all the earth! —Psalm 96:1 (RSV)

FROM THE FIRST DAY my mother-in-law came into my life, we were soul mates, bound by our love for her son. She called me "daughter," never "daughter-in-law."

In the early days of our relationship, she would assure me of her support in ways other than words. Once I came to dinner to find a pink washcloth rolled and tied with a ribbon by the side of my plate. The next time it was a special book. She found a hundred ways to serve cantaloupe, my favorite fruit.

When my husband, Gary, and I moved to New York, her love was set down in scores of letters. She made a poem on the birth of her grandson Timothy, which she copied painstakingly on a fancy card. For his third birthday, she hand-lettered a story on squares of felt and bound it with a needlepoint cover. His grandmother was "Nana, the storyteller," spinning tales of coal mines and timberland where family heroes had labored.

Her words took on new urgency when she fell ill. "I love you, hon," she declared at the end of

6
WEDNESDAY

"If we are thrown into the blazing furnace, the God we serve is able to deliver us from it . . . . But even if he does not . . . we will not serve your gods or worship the image of gold you have set up." —Daniel 3:17–18 (NIV)

7
THURSDAY

She hath done what she could . . . . —Mark 14:8 (KJV)

8
FRIDAY

"His master replied, 'Well done, good and faithful servant! You have been faithful with a few things; I will put you in charge of many things. Come and share your master's happiness!'" —Matthew 25:23 (NIV)

9
SATURDAY

Oh, the depth of the riches and wisdom and knowledge of God! How unsearchable are his judgments and how inscrutable his ways! —Romans 11:33 (ESV)

---

each phone conversation. Even her last, when she could barely speak.

I hear her still.

—*Linda Ching Sledge*

PRAYER REQUESTS _____

_____

_____

_____

JANUARY

S	M	T	W	T	F	S
					1	2
3	4	5	6	7	8	9
10	11	12	13	14	15	16
17	18	19	20	21	22	23
24/31	25	26	27	28	29	30

OUR PRAYER

You have created us to be different for reasons, God. Help us to see those differences and then learn from them instead of dismissing them.

10
SUNDAY

"Choose the good." —Isaiah 7:15 (KJV)

11
MONDAY

Then he opened their minds so they could understand the Scriptures. —Luke 24:45 (NIV)

12
TUESDAY

"Surely the Lord is in this place . . . ." —Genesis 28:16 (NIV)

ALABAMA IS AN AGRICULTURAL STATE. Most homeowners have small vegetable gardens, and we look to our county services office for advice on planting and growing.

A New Year's greeting that our service sent suggested the way to plant a most successful garden this year. I plan to dig in and get mine started. Perhaps you'll want to do so too.

Here, with a bit of paraphrasing, is the layout for planting:

PLANT FOUR ROWS OF PEAS (P'S)
Prayer, Promptness, Patience, Preparation

PLANT FOUR ROWS OF SQUASH
Squash gossip, *Squash* indifference, *Squash* criticism, *Squash* negative thinking

PLANT FOUR ROWS OF TURNIPS (TURN UPS)
Turn up for church services, *Turn up* whenever needed, *Turn up* with a friendly smile, *Turn up*

13
WEDNESDAY

Even the darkness will not be dark to you; the night will shine like the day, for darkness is as light to you. —Psalm 139:12 (NIV)

14
THURSDAY

Then God said, "Let us make humankind in our image, according to our likeness . . . ." —Genesis 1:26 (NRSV)

15
FRIDAY

. . . And after the earthquake, a fire, but the Lord was not in the fire; and after the fire a still small voice. —1 Kings 19:12 (NKJV)

16
SATURDAY

The Lord is good to all, and His mercies are over all His works. —Psalm 145:9 (NAS)

with determination to be a better person

Cultivate well, keep saturated with love, and reap a harvest of peace and happiness. Lots of good luck in your garden this year!

—Drue Duke

PRAYER REQUESTS _____

_____

_____

_____

JANUARY

S	M	T	W	T	F	S
					1	2
3	4	5	6	7	8	9
10	11	12	13	14	15	16
17	18	19	20	21	22	23
24/31	25	26	27	28	29	30

OUR PRAYER

Let me be still, Father. Let me meet You here, now.

17
SUNDAY

Therefore, since we have been justified by faith, we have peace with God through our Lord Jesus Christ. —Romans 5:1 (ESV)

18
MONDAY

MARTIN
LUTHER KING
JR. DAY

How good and pleasant it is when God's people live together in unity! —Psalm 133:1 (NIV)

19
TUESDAY

Ye are all the children of God by faith in Christ Jesus. For as many of you as have been baptized into Christ have put on Christ. —Galatians 3:26–27 (KJV)

My husband and I were tempted to throw the tiny blue and gold grandfather clock out with the trash. It wouldn't keep the right time. In spite of all the careful adjustments made on the delicate two-inch pendulum and the meticulous balancing of the little weight fastened to its stem, the timepiece ticked off the minutes as though it couldn't wait for tomorrow.

And then my husband became seriously ill. His hospitalization lasted many weeks, and for a while it seemed that he might never come home. At first, the loneliness of my days was unbearable. While I waited, praying desperately for God's help, the little clock continued to tick gaily along. It seemed to be racing ahead, singing out, "It won't be long! He'll soon be home! It won't be long!" As I prayed, the sound comforted me and gave me courage.

My husband recovered and is home again. The willful little clock still doesn't keep time.

20
WEDNESDAY

"I will bring healing to you and cure you . . . ." —Jeremiah 30:17 (JPS)

21
THURSDAY

"The Lord is my helper; I will not fear. What can man do to me?" —Hebrews 13:6 (NKJV)

22
FRIDAY

"Be still . . . ." —Psalm 46:10 (KJV)

23
SATURDAY

Do not be conformed to this world, but be transformed by the renewal of your mind . . . .
—Romans 12:2 (ESV)

However, I wind it regularly, for the sound of its ticking has become a source of hope for me and a reminder that God, Who is never far away, sometimes uses strange devices to comfort us.

—Doris Haase

PRAYER REQUESTS _____

_____

_____

_____

JANUARY

S	M	T	W	T	F	S
					1	2
3	4	5	6	7	8	9
10	11	12	13	14	15	16
17	18	19	20	21	22	23
24/31	25	26	27	28	29	30

OUR PRAYER

*Help me to discern, Lord, between keeping things
for greed or for good, and that my true treasures are
awaiting me in heaven, not on earth.*

24
SUNDAY

Woe unto you, scribes and Pharisees, hypocrites! for ye pay tithe of mint and anise and cummin, and have omitted the weightier matters of the law, judgment, mercy, and faith . . . Ye blind guides, which strain at a gnat, and swallow a camel. —Matthew 23:23–24 (KJV)

25
MONDAY

"Therefore I tell you, do not worry about your life . . . ." —Matthew 6:25 (NIV)

26
TUESDAY

The law written in their hearts, their conscience also bearing witness . . . .
—Romans 2:15 (KJV)

THE TEARS ROLLED STEADILY down her face and dripped onto her blouse, making a dark mark. We were standing around the Communion table at an early morning service, and I didn't know if her tears came from sorrow or from the wonder of worship. I had never seen her before. Big city churches welcome many strangers.

I am both reserved and shy—foolish at this stage in my life, but a fact. So it surprised—almost shocked—me to see my hand stretch out and take hers. The serene voices of the choir continued to sing:

Here I am, Lord.
Is it I, Lord?
I have heard You calling in the night.

The weeping stranger and I held hands. The hymn ended. The congregation greeted one another. She squeezed my hand, whispered "Thank you," and walked out of my life.

Afterward, I thought about those few moments. I wondered what gave me the confidence to reach out and take her hand. I just never do things like

27
WEDNESDAY

For now we see through a glass, darkly; but then face to face . . . .
—1 Corinthians 13:12 (KJV)

28
THURSDAY

"For the Lord searches every heart and understands every desire and every thought . . . ."
—1 Chronicles 28:9 (NIV)

29
FRIDAY

Do not lay up for yourselves treasures on earth, where moth and rust destroy . . . .
—Matthew 6:19 (NKJV)

30
SATURDAY

Have mercy on me, O God, because of your unfailing love. Because of your great compassion, blot out the stain of my sins. —Psalm 51:1 (NLT)

that; I never ask questions at lectures or offer my opinion unsolicited.

But the explanation is so simple. I was in God's house, and when you're in someone's house, you follow house rules.

—*Brigitte Weeks*

PRAYER REQUESTS _____

_____

_____

_____

JANUARY

S	M	T	W	T	F	S
					1	2
3	4	5	6	7	8	9
10	11	12	13	14	15	16
17	18	19	20	21	22	23
24/31	25	26	27	28	29	30

Thou shalt not make unto thee any graven image.... —EXODUS 20:4 (KJV)

A PRAYER FOR FEBRUARY

Give me, O Lord,
a steadfast heart,
which no unworthy affection
may drag downwards;
give me an unconquered heart,
which no tribulation
can wear out;
give me an upright heart,
which no unworthy purpose
may tempt aside.

THOMAS AQUINAS (1225–1274)

THE SECOND COMMANDMENT

God,
When I think of graven images
I think of golden calves
wooden statues
saints of stone.
And I know I'll never bow
To one of these.
So I find it easy
To follow Your commandment.

But wait…
What about those other things
That people seem to worship
Like money,
beauty,
the power of the mind—
Images not carved of stone or clay
But sculpted, insidiously,
Inside the heart.

O Creator, keep my adoration image free.
There cannot be another god for me.

FEBRUARY 2016

SUNDAY	MONDAY	TUESDAY	WEDNESDAY	THURSDAY	FRIDAY	SATURDAY
	1	2	3	4	5	6
7	8	9	10 ASH WEDNESDAY	11	12 ABRAHAM LINCOLN'S BIRTHDAY	13
14 VALENTINE'S DAY	15 PRESIDENTS' DAY	16	17	18	19	20
21	22 GEORGE WASHINGTON'S BIRTHDAY	23	24	25	26	27
28	29					

NOTES

JANUARY

S	M	T	W	T	F	S
					1	2
3	4	5	6	7	8	9
10	11	12	13	14	15	16
17	18	19	20	21	22	23
24/31	25	26	27	28	29	30

MARCH

S	M	T	W	T	F	S
		1	2	3	4	5
6	7	8	9	10	11	12
13	14	15	16	17	18	19
20	21	22	23	24	25	26
27	28	29	30	31		

OUR PRAYER

Father, thank You for biology and microscopes and tiny creeping things. And help me to see what is excellent and praiseworthy in them all.

31
SUNDAY

Your face, Lord, I will seek. —Psalm 27:8 (NIV)

FEBRUARY

1
MONDAY

Being confident of this, that he who began a good work in you will carry it on to completion until the day of Christ Jesus. —Philippians 1:6 (NIV)

2
TUESDAY

Whoever serves, as one who serves by the strength that God supplies—in order that in everything God may be glorified through Jesus Christ . . . . —1 Peter 4:11 (ESV)

"It's a boy!" our son Pat announced excitedly before I'd finished muttering a groggy "hello" into the telephone receiver. Ryan Patrick, our first grandchild, had entered the world at 3:45 AM. A few hours later, I held him in my arms—surely, the most beautiful baby in the world!

As I drove home from the hospital late that night, I replayed our first meeting, visualizing every detail of Ryan's tiny body, recalling every burp and yawn and cry, enjoying again the feel of him snuggled against my shoulder. We had been waiting for this child with a wonderful sense of anticipation. I thought I knew what it would be like when he arrived, but I was not prepared for my strong feelings when I held him for the first time.

God's love became more than an abstract concept, more than a promise from Scripture. With Ryan in my arms, God's love became a tangible, touchable presence. I knew with absolute certainty

3
WEDNESDAY

"Even to your old age I am he, and to gray hairs I will carry you. I have made, and I will bear; I will carry and will save." —Isaiah 46:4 (ESV)

4
THURSDAY

"And the Word was made flesh . . . full of grace and truth." —John 1:14 (KJV)

5
FRIDAY

Whatever is pure, whatever is lovely, whatever is admirable— if anything is excellent or praiseworthy—think about such things. —Philippians 4:8 (NIV)

6
SATURDAY

The eternal God is your refuge, and his everlasting arms are under you. —Deuteronomy 33:27 (NLT)

that God loved me, and I praise and thank God with my whole heart for using another baby, born on a cold January day, to reassure me of that real love.

—*Penney Schwab*

PRAYER REQUESTS _____

_____

_____

_____

FEBRUARY

S	M	T	W	T	F	S
	1	2	3	4	5	6
7	8	9	10	11	12	13
14	15	16	17	18	19	20
21	22	23	24	25	26	27
28	29					

OUR PRAYER

God of celebration, remind us how our
stories and songs come together in You.

7
SUNDAY

Search me, O God, and know my heart: try me, and know my thoughts: And see if there be any wicked way in me, and lead me in the way everlasting. —Psalm 139:23–24 (KJV)

8
MONDAY

"With all our tribulation and in spite of it, I am filled with comfort. . . ." —2 Corinthians 7:4 (AMP)

9
TUESDAY

"Lord, to whom shall we go? You have the words of eternal life." —John 6:68 (NIV)

WHEN OUR DAUGHTER MEGHAN left home to attend college, she did not join a church and fell in with students who did not share her spiritual values. When she came to visit us during semester break, she admitted she was lonely and depressed, her grades were falling, and she was considering quitting school.

After she had returned to classes, I couldn't sleep for worrying. "Lord," I prayed, "she's so vulnerable right now. I know You're with her, but please, she needs an earthly friend to encourage her too."

An answer came almost as if God had tapped me on the shoulder: *You must be that friend.*

So I bought a stack of postcards with scenes to remind her of home. I wrote personal messages and included a corresponding Bible verse. "I will never leave thee, nor forsake thee" (Hebrews 13:5) was one I sent.

Meghan did stay in school, her grades came

10
WEDNESDAY

ASH
WEDNESDAY

"I, I am he who blots out your transgressions for my own sake, and I will not remember your sins." —Isaiah 43:25 (ESV)

11
THURSDAY

The Lord is my strength and song. . . . —Exodus 15:2 (KJV)

12
FRIDAY

ABRAHAM
LINCOLN'S
BIRTHDAY

"I will sing a new song to you, O God; upon a ten-stringed harp I will play to you." —Psalm 144:9 (NRSV)

13
SATURDAY

In all circumstances take up the shield of faith, with which you can extinguish all the flaming darts of the evil one; and take the helmet of salvation, and the sword of the Spirit, which is the word of God. —Ephesians 6:16–17 (ESV)

back up, and eventually she found not only a church home but new friends with whom she could be happy. She went on to graduate with two degrees and today she counsels troubled teenagers.

—*Madge Harrah*

PRAYER REQUESTS _____

_____

_____

_____

FEBRUARY

S	M	T	W	T	F	S
	1	2	3	4	5	6
7	8	9	10	11	12	13
14	15	16	17	18	19	20
21	22	23	24	25	26	27
28	29					

OUR PRAYER

I'll let You do the talking when I pray today, Lord.
Speak to me in the beauty of Your creation.

14
SUNDAY

VALENTINE'S DAY

How precious is your steadfast love, O God! —Psalm 36:7 (ESV)

15
MONDAY

PRESIDENTS' DAY

The Lord has anointed me to bring good news to the afflicted; He has sent me to bind up the brokenhearted, to proclaim liberty to captives and freedom to prisoners. . . . —Isaiah 61:1 (NAS)

16
TUESDAY

Enter his gates with thanksgiving, and his courts with praise! —Psalm 100:4 (ESV)

SOMETIMES WHEN I ATTEND CHURCH, I feel as if I'm cuddling right up to God. Yet when I leave the sanctuary and step back into the world, I get so caught up in my life and commitments that it seems as if I left God behind in church.

And nowhere is my faith more sorely tested than when I get behind the steering wheel. I demand my rights and bristle at drivers who cut me off or pass me to gain a car's length or turn without signaling. Having little or no patience, I let them know of my annoyance with a blast on the horn.

But the Scriptures say I'm to turn the other cheek, return good for evil, and forgive seventy times seven. So what am I supposed to do? Turn the other fender? Maybe I should walk or let my wife drive.

But down deep in my heart, a voice tells me that God will ride with me, help me brake and

17
WEDNESDAY

Jacob . . . lay down. . . . And he dreamed that there was a ladder set up on the earth, the top of it reaching to heaven; and the angels of God were ascending and descending on it. And the Lord stood beside him. . . . —Genesis 28:10–13 (NRSV)

18
THURSDAY

"The promise is for you and your children and for all who are far off — for all whom the Lord our God will call." —Acts 2:39 (NIV)

19
FRIDAY

"Holy, holy, holy is the Lord of hosts; the whole earth is full of his glory." —Isaiah 6:3 (NRSV)

20
SATURDAY

When pride comes, so does shame, but wisdom brings humility. —Proverbs 11:2 (CEB)

steer, and anoint me with a special peace that will enable me to handle any eventuality with love. I guess it's one way I'm learning to bring God with me into my world, Monday through Saturday too.

—Sam Justice

PRAYER REQUESTS _____

_____

_____

_____

FEBRUARY

S	M	T	W	T	F	S
	1	2	3	4	5	6
7	8	9	10	11	12	13
14	15	16	17	18	19	20
21	22	23	24	25	26	27
28	29					

OUR PRAYER

Lord, spare us from clichés and platitudes
so that we may know each other's hearts.

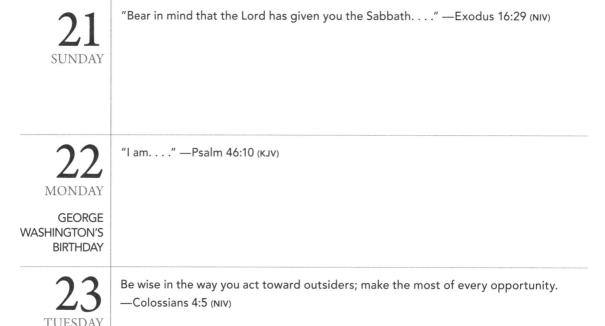

21
SUNDAY

"Bear in mind that the Lord has given you the Sabbath. . . ." —Exodus 16:29 (NIV)

22
MONDAY

GEORGE
WASHINGTON'S
BIRTHDAY

"I am. . . ." —Psalm 46:10 (KJV)

23
TUESDAY

Be wise in the way you act toward outsiders; make the most of every opportunity.
—Colossians 4:5 (NIV)

LAST WINTER I WAS ILL with the flu and went to my doctor. He gave me a shot and some pills, telling me to take four of them every two hours. I decided it was too much medicine and that I would take two pills every four hours. Soon I was feeling a little better. Days passed, though, and my illness dragged on. I didn't feel too bad, but I wasn't well. I returned to my doctor and told him my opinions about taking so much medicine. He was disappointed with me.

"If you had followed my directions, that much medication would have killed those germs. You are just making them mad and giving them a chance to build up immunity against the pills. I can't help you if you won't trust me and follow my directions exactly!"

I must also give myself to God completely, holding nothing back, if I am to have the

24
WEDNESDAY

Look to the Lord and his strength; seek his face always. —1 Chronicles 16:11 (NIV)

25
THURSDAY

But you are a chosen generation, a royal priesthood, a holy nation, His own special people, that you may proclaim the praises of Him who called you out of darkness into His marvelous light. —1 Peter 2:9 (NKJV)

26
FRIDAY

Now therefore, listen to me, my children; pay attention to the words of my mouth. . . . —Proverbs 7:24 (NKJV)

27
SATURDAY

Let perseverance finish its work so that you may be mature and complete, not lacking anything. —James 1:4 (NIV)

most joyous, successful life God means for me. God wants me to trust—body, mind, and soul. When I fully dedicate myself to God, then I reap the full, joyous benefits of God's love and blessing.

—Lucille Campbell

PRAYER REQUESTS _____

_____

_____

_____

FEBRUARY

S	M	T	W	T	F	S
	1	2	3	4	5	6
7	8	9	10	11	12	13
14	15	16	17	18	19	20
21	22	23	24	25	26	27
28	29					

A PRAYER FOR MARCH

Hallowed be Thy name, not mine,
Thy Kingdom come, not mine,
Thy will be done, not mine,
Give us peace with Thee,
Peace with men,
Peace with ourselves,
And free us from all fear.

DAG HAMMARSKJÖLD (1905–1961)

THE THIRD COMMANDMENT

Last week
I answered the door
And there was another salesman.
"Oh, God," I said out loud,
"I don't need a brush!"
And firmly told him so.

I meant it about the brush, God,
But I never meant to use Your name
That way—as my outlet
for exasperation.
Surely You know
How mindless it is,
How everybody does it…
but…then…here I am
Making excuses when
All the while I know I'm wrong.
You've set it down
so simply and so clearly,
Your name, Your precious name,
I should not take in vain.

The next time I say
"Oh, God,"
I won't stop there.
I'll make it be a prayer
That starts
"Oh, God…how great Thou art!"
For how really great
Thou art.

❧ MARCH 2016 ❧

SUNDAY	MONDAY	TUESDAY	WEDNESDAY	THURSDAY	FRIDAY	SATURDAY
		1	2	3	4	5
6	7	8	9	10	11	12
13 DAYLIGHT SAVING TIME BEGINS	14	15	16	17 ST. PATRICK'S DAY	18	19
20 PALM SUNDAY / SPRING BEGINS	21	22	23	24 MAUNDY THURSDAY	25 GUIDEPOSTS GOOD FRIDAY DAY OF PRAYER	26
27 EASTER	28	29	30	31		

NOTES

FEBRUARY

S	M	T	W	T	F	S
	1	2	3	4	5	6
7	8	9	10	11	12	13
14	15	16	17	18	19	20
21	22	23	24	25	26	27
28	29					

APRIL

S	M	T	W	T	F	S
					1	2
3	4	5	6	7	8	9
10	11	12	13	14	15	16
17	18	19	20	21	22	23
24	25	26	27	28	29	30

OUR PRAYER

Dear Lord, when doubt and questions trouble me,
help me to have faith that there are reasons
I'm not to know right now.

28
SUNDAY

Even so the body is not made up of one part but of many. —1 Corinthians 12:14 (NIV)

29
MONDAY

One of his disciples said to him, "Lord, teach us to pray. . . ." —Luke 11:1 (NIV)

MARCH

1
TUESDAY

He has told you, O mortal, what is good; and what does the Lord require of you but to do justice, and to love kindness, and to walk humbly with your God? —Micah 6:8 (NRSV)

"Remember," our pastor said as he concluded the sermon, "worship is every bit as important to your spiritual well-being as breathing is to your physical health."

While he gave the closing prayer, I mentally reviewed the introduction to the last hymn. As I played the organ, a familiar feeling of guilt accompanied every note. I had a secret: although I attended church every Sunday, I didn't worship. I was too busy concentrating on the details of the service.

Finally, I confessed this to a friend. Her response was not what I expected. "Why do you think it's called the worship *service*?" she asked. "Because for many of us—the pastor, the acolytes, the musicians—it's a time to *serve*. We worship through our work. Still, it's important to find times when you're free of responsibility and can give your whole heart to worship."

I began to seek a few nontraditional opportunities for worship: an evangelism event, musical presentations, even an occasional TV service. And a

2
WEDNESDAY

"Trust in the Lord with all your heart . . . ." —Proverbs 3:5 (NIV)

3
THURSDAY

"For where two or three are gathered in my name, there am I among them."
—Matthew 18:20 (ESV)

4
FRIDAY

Jesus replied, "You don't understand now what I am doing, but someday you will."
—John 13:7 (NLT)

5
SATURDAY

For by me your days will be multiplied, and years will be added to your life.
—Proverbs 9:11 (NRSV)

strange thing happened: although most Sunday mornings still find me on the organ bench, and every head is bowed and every eye closed except mine, there are plenty of times now when worship happens.

—*Penney Schwab*

PRAYER REQUESTS _____

_____

_____

_____

MARCH

S	M	T	W	T	F	S
		1	2	3	4	5
6	7	8	9	10	11	12
13	14	15	16	17	18	19
20	21	22	23	24	25	26
27	28	29	30	31		

Lord, letting go of those I love is hard.
Thank You for setting the example for how to do it.

6
SUNDAY

For we walk by faith, not by sight. —2 Corinthians 5:7 (NRSV)

7
MONDAY

When you lie down, you will not be afraid . . . your sleep will be sweet.
—Proverbs 3:24 (NIV)

8
TUESDAY

For where your treasure is, there your heart will be also. —Matthew 6:21 (ESV)

THE WOMAN, BY HER DRESS, appeared to be a Muslim. I was in Croatia to visit Christians forced from their homes and was traveling alone to a town I knew nothing about, except that it had a hotel. No one was due to meet me there until the next day.

"Follow her," I was told by the others in the six-person train compartment as we neared the stop. "She has a car and will take you to your hotel." So I followed her to a small, battered, Russian-made Lada and we drove the three miles in

silence. Suddenly, two blocks from the hotel, she pulled the car to the side of the street and nodded her head to the door. I got out and trudged those last two blocks through the swirling snow and biting wind.

When I mentioned it to the hotel clerk, she asked, "Did you know that woman risked her life for you? If anyone had seen you in that car, she would have been severely punished. Our culture is different from yours. Keep that in mind."

I did, but never more clearly than when I came

9
WEDNESDAY

"Whenever you did one of these things to someone overlooked or ignored, that was me—you did it to me." —Matthew 25:40 (MSG)

10
THURSDAY

"I have lift up mine hand unto the Lord . . . . —Genesis 14:22 (KJV)

11
FRIDAY

Now, our God, we give you thanks, and praise your glorious name. —1 Chronicles 29:13 (NIV)

12
SATURDAY

Great is his faithfulness; his mercies begin afresh each morning. —Lamentations 3:23 (NLT)

across the story of the Good Samaritan. The vast difference between cultures of the Samaritan and the one he helped was a huge risk. But he did, like the Muslim woman in Croatia who took a big risk to help a stranger.

—Jeff Japinga

PRAYER REQUESTS _____

_____

_____

_____

MARCH

S	M	T	W	T	F	S
		1	2	3	4	5
6	7	8	9	10	11	12
13	14	15	16	17	18	19
20	21	22	23	24	25	26
27	28	29	30	31		

OUR PRAYER

*Father, I pray for Your love as
the ultimate healing answer. Amen.*

13
SUNDAY

DAYLIGHT
SAVING TIME
BEGINS

Moses said, "Eat this today, because today is the Sabbath, a day of rest dedicated to the Lord, and you will not find any food outside the camp. You must gather food for six days, but on the seventh day, the day of rest, there will be none." —Exodus 16:25–26 (GNT)

14
MONDAY

For everyone born of God overcomes the world. . . . —1 John 5:4 (NIV)

15
TUESDAY

"Peace I leave with you. My peace I give you. I give to you not as the world gives. Don't be troubled or afraid." —John 14:27 (CEB)

I'll never forget the first job I ever had. Just fourteen years old, I was being paid eleven dollars a week to be a salesclerk at the ribbon counter of a department store. Eleven dollars didn't seem like much, so I asked for a raise. The manager said he would think about it.

One day a most disagreeable customer appeared at my counter. She rummaged through the ribbon display, finding nothing that pleased her, and grumbled and complained about everything. I had been told to remember that "the customer is always right," so I kept my temper and tried to be as polite and helpful as possible. But I was thankful when she moved on.

Later that day the manager called me in to his office. To my delight, he said my salary was being raised to a princely thirteen dollars. The reason, he went on, was my performance with the unpleasant customer. "We use her sometimes to test our employees' patience and self-control. We told her to be as difficult with you as possible. I'm glad to say you passed the test."

16
WEDNESDAY

After fasting forty days and forty nights, he was hungry. —Matthew 4:2 (NIV)

17
THURSDAY

ST. PATRICK'S DAY

But I say unto you, Love your enemies. . . . —Matthew 5:44 (KJV)

18
FRIDAY

Jesus said unto her, I am the resurrection and the life: he that believeth in me, though he were dead, yet shall he live. —John 11:25 (KJV)

19
SATURDAY

"Then Simon Peter came along behind him and went straight into the tomb. . . ." —John 20:6 (NIV)

Patience and *self-control*. I wonder sometimes if life doesn't test us all for these qualities. Certainly each time we pass the test we get a "raise:" a raise in the opinion of others, a raise in our own self-esteem, and most important of all, a raise in the sight of God.

—*Ruth Stafford Peale*

PRAYER REQUESTS _____

_____

_____

_____

MARCH

S	M	T	W	T	F	S
		1	2	3	4	5
6	7	8	9	10	11	12
13	14	15	16	17	18	19
20	21	22	23	24	25	26
27	28	29	30	31		

OUR PRAYER
Lord, help me to remember the pain of Good Friday
and to never forget the victory of Easter.

---

20 SUNDAY

PALM SUNDAY
SPRING BEGINS

"If you are offering your gift at the altar and there remember that your brother has something against you. . . . go and be reconciled to your brother. . . ." —Matthew 5:23–24 (NIV)

---

21 MONDAY

"I . . . enabled you to walk with heads held high." —Leviticus 26:13 (NIV)

---

22 TUESDAY

"And he was healed from that moment." —Matthew 17:18 (NIV)

I WAS RAISED TO BELIEVE that Good Friday is the saddest day in the history of the world, yet I have discovered a certain joy in it.

I was not aware of this gift until I went to Tanzania, and some missionaries told me about a very old man who lived nearby and came to the mission every day to teach religion to the schoolchildren. "He is a saint. You must meet him."

He turned out to be a short man, lean, slightly stooped, his face all wrinkles, but his eyes and mind bright and alert. I could see he was a happy man. At one point, I asked him which aspect of his faith he valued most. Without hesitation he said, "The forgiveness of sin."

Since meeting that African, I have never lived through this very special day without thinking of his words of joy. And I am sure now that if I had been able to observe Jesus during the last week of His life on earth, even if I had not been persuaded by His miracles and His teachings, I

23 WEDNESDAY

"Others cut branches from the tress and spread them on the road." —Matthew 21:8 (NIV)

24 THURSDAY

MAUNDY THURRSDAY

I will praise God's name in song and glorify him with thanksgiving. —Psalm 69:30 (NIV)

25 FRIDAY

GUIDEPOSTS GOOD FRIDAY DAY OF PRAYER

"Pray for the peace of Jerusalem . . . ." —Psalm 122:6 (NIV)

26 SATURDAY

"Go," he told him, "wash in the Pool of Siloam . . . ." So the man went and washed, and came home seeing." —John 9:7 (NIV)

certainly would have given Him my life after hearing His burst of loving forgiveness on the Cross.

Maybe that is why we call this saddest day in history *Good* Friday.

—*Glenn Kittler*

PRAYER REQUESTS _____

_____

_____

_____

MARCH

S	M	T	W	T	F	S
		1	2	3	4	5
6	7	8	9	10	11	12
13	14	15	16	17	18	19
20	21	22	23	24	25	26
27	28	29	30	31		

27
SUNDAY

EASTER

"Where is the guest room, where I may eat the Passover with my disciples?"
—Luke 22:11 (NIV)

28
MONDAY

"Watch and pray . . . . The spirit is willing, but the body is weak." —Matthew 26:41 (NIV)

29
TUESDAY

"I know every bird of the mountains, and everything that moves in the field is Mine."
—Psalm 50:11 (NAS)

WHAT A JOY it must have been for Jesus to appear to His friends after His Resurrection. I see this joy coming out in the covert encounter with two discouraged disciples who were shuffling their way toward Emmaus. Incognito, Jesus joins them and pretends not to know what they are talking about.

"What things?" He asks, as if He didn't know. He listens sympathetically and reminds them of some Scriptures they had overlooked. When, at last, He reveals himself, their hearts once again burn with hope.

It's all too easy to lose hope in this life, I think. That dream job gets put on the back burner because you need cash now. The handsome prince you married turns out to be a toad. Someone else bought the split-level you wanted, and college plans were set aside when the children came along.

The Resurrection of Christ is a wake-up call for my sidetracked yearnings. When God is involved,

30
WEDNESDAY

Your Father knows what you need before you ask him. —Matthew 6:8 (NIV)

31
THURSDAY

Hast thou entered into the treasures of the snow? . . . —Job 38:22 (KJV)

APRIL

1
FRIDAY

"For with God nothing will be impossible." —Luke 1:37 (NKJV)

2
SATURDAY

"I needed clothes and you clothed me. . . ." —Matthew 25:36 (NIV)

there is always hope. Hope is not just a noun, it's also a verb.

Easter, the anniversary of death's defeat, would be a good time to dust off one of those dreams and present it to the Lord of Hope.

—*Daniel Schantz*

PRAYER REQUESTS _____

_____

_____

_____

MARCH

S	M	T	W	T	F	S
		1	2	3	4	5
6	7	8	9	10	11	12
13	14	15	16	17	18	19
20	21	22	23	24	25	26
27	28	29	30	31		

THE FOURTH COMMANDMENT

What once was called the sabbath
is now a long weekend.
What once was called a holy day
is thought of as a holiday.
Strange, isn't it, how we alter things,
forgetting—or ignoring—
the reason for their being?

O God, You said
The sabbath was made for humankind,
And so it is;
But now I work so hard at play
I tire myself for labor days.

Remind me, God,
Tell me again,
That even You required a time
to rest and be renewed.
Now when I hurry through the sabbath day,
Stop me!
Stop me and let me know
That You, the mighty one,
expect a great deal more from me
than just a fleeting nod.

A PRAYER FOR APRIL

Incline us O God!
to think humbly of
ourselves, to be saved
only in the examination
of our own conduct,
to consider
our fellow creatures
with kindness,
and to judge of all they say
and do with the charity
which we would desire
from them ourselves.

JANE AUSTEN (1775–1817)

❋ APRIL 2016 ❈

SUNDAY	MONDAY	TUESDAY	WEDNESDAY	THURSDAY	FRIDAY	SATURDAY
					1	2
3	4	5	6	7	8	9
10	11	12	13	14	15	16
17	18	19	20	21	22 EARTH DAY	23 PASSOVER
24	25	26	27	28	29	30

NOTES

MARCH

S	M	T	W	T	F	S
		1	2	3	4	5
6	7	8	9	10	11	12
13	14	15	16	17	18	19
20	21	22	23	24	25	26
27	28	29	30	31		

MAY

S	M	T	W	T	F	S
1	2	3	4	5	6	7
8	9	10	11	12	13	14
15	16	17	18	19	20	21
22	23	24	25	26	27	28
29	30	31				

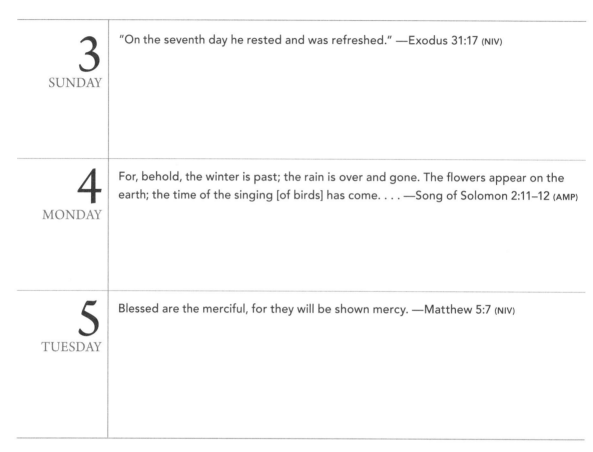

3
SUNDAY

"On the seventh day he rested and was refreshed." —Exodus 31:17 (NIV)

4
MONDAY

For, behold, the winter is past; the rain is over and gone. The flowers appear on the earth; the time of the singing [of birds] has come. . . . —Song of Solomon 2:11–12 (AMP)

5
TUESDAY

Blessed are the merciful, for they will be shown mercy. —Matthew 5:7 (NIV)

MORNING RUSH HOUR, and the subway car was a sardine can of half-awake New Yorkers. It was raining, dampening spirits as well as skins. Under the roar of the train, I imagined I could hear rumbles of discontent.

Trapped and unable to move, I found myself staring into the frowning face of a young woman. As she glanced over my shoulder, the frown vanished and a smile tugged at her lips. The same thing happened to the young man standing next to her and to the old man beside him and to the college student glancing up from her book. All started to look over my shoulder and smile.

I turned around to see what they were looking at and began to smile too. Above the door, some graffiti artist had proclaimed: I LOV EVRY SINGEL BODDY IN THE HOLE WORLD.

Kid, I thought, *you can't spell and you shouldn't write on subway cars, but you've certainly got the right idea.*

6
WEDNESDAY

So you see, faith by itself isn't enough. Unless it produces good deeds, it is dead and useless. —James 2:17 (NLT)

7
THURSDAY

"Guard against every kind of greed. Life is not measured by how much you own." —Luke 12:15 (NLT)

8
FRIDAY

Truly, I say to you, whoever does not receive the kingdom of God like a child shall not enter it. —Mark 10:15 (ESV)

9
SATURDAY

And if the root be holy, so are the branches. —Romans 11:16 (KJV)

I thought of other sullen moments when a smile or a friendly nod could have chased away my inner storms. Perhaps, if it came from me, I could do as much for others. It's worth trying. Don't you agree?
—*Glenn Kittler*

PRAYER REQUESTS _____

_____

_____

_____

APRIL

S	M	T	W	T	F	S
					1	2
3	4	5	6	7	8	9
10	11	12	13	14	15	16
17	18	19	20	21	22	23
24	25	26	27	28	29	30

10
SUNDAY

Come near to God and he will come near to you. Wash your hands, you sinners, and purify your hearts. . . . —James 4:8 (NIV)

11
MONDAY

If ye have faith as a grain of mustard seed . . . nothing shall be impossible unto you. —Matthew 17:20 (KJV)

12
TUESDAY

And the sash of fine twined linen and of blue and purple and scarlet yarns, embroidered with needlework, as the Lord had commanded Moses. —Exodus 39:29 (ESV)

DID YOU EVER NOTICE how a cat isn't satisfied unless it's touching you? Baby, our new chocolate-brown Burmese, is no exception. He came to us when a friend was transferred abroad to a country with strict quarantine laws.

Lonely for his old family and afraid of his new surroundings, Baby wouldn't come near us for two days. He'd hide under the sofa, until we pulled him out and stroked him. Now he isn't content unless he rubs against our legs or curls up on top of us, rubbing his head against whatever part of us he can reach.

People need the security of a touch too. When I visit a sick friend in the hospital, she may be glad to have company. But if I hold her hand, the bond of friendship is much stronger. I can stand up straight and tell my son that I love him, but if I stoop to put my arms around him, he knows I mean it.

Jesus went from town to town touching people—healing them, encouraging them, lov-

13
WEDNESDAY

"Consider the lilies, how they grow: they neither toil nor spin; yet I tell you, even Solomon in all his glory was not clothed like one of these." —Luke 12:27 (NRSV)

14
THURSDAY

For everything created by God is good, and nothing is to be rejected, provided it is received with thanksgiving. —1 Timothy 4:4 (NRSV)

15
FRIDAY

"Whom the Lord loveth he correcteth; even as a father the son in whom he delighteth." —Proverbs 3:12 (KJV)

16
SATURDAY

Remember the sabbath day, and keep it holy. . . . For in six days the Lord made heaven and earth, the sea and all that is in them, but rested the seventh day; therefore the Lord blessed the sabbath day and consecrated it. —Exodus 20:8, 11 (NRSV)

ing them. One woman found new life by touching merely the hem of His robe. His arms are ever outstretched to you and me. Take hold of them today—and that of someone near you—and let Jesus's love flow through.

—*Betty R. Graham*

PRAYER REQUESTS _____

_____

_____

_____

APRIL

S	M	T	W	T	F	S
					1	2
3	4	5	6	7	8	9
10	11	12	13	14	15	16
17	18	19	20	21	22	23
24	25	26	27	28	29	30

17
SUNDAY

"For You said, 'I will surely prosper you and make your descendants as the sand of the sea, which is too great to be numbered.'" —Genesis 32:12 (NAS)

18
MONDAY

Little children, let us stop just saying we love people; let us really love them, and show it by our actions. —1 John 3:18 (TLB)

19
TUESDAY

You surround me with songs of deliverance —Psalm 32:7 (NAS)

I WALKED INTO our little church earlier than usual and noticed dusty footprints covered the foyer rug, crumpled bulletins scattered under the sanctuary pews, and hymnbooks askew in their racks. A deaconess who was hastily tidying up stopped to apologize. "I'm afraid there was a mix-up in the schedule, and as a result the church didn't get cleaned."

"Let me help," I said as I removed my coat.

Whisking our way through the sanctuary, we straightened hymnals, and I wondered, *When was the last time I spontaneously made a joyful noise unto the Lord?* We picked up stray bulletins, and I recalled how I'd been dropping quite a few quiet times lately. We erased blackboards as I prayed, *Lord, I'm having a hard time wiping away a past hurt.* We picked up scraps of paper and crayons, and I asked forgiveness for picturing a certain person in a bad light. We straightened chairs. *Haven't I shoved aside a good intention recently?* Finally, we agreed that the dusty footprints on the foyer rug would have to stay for now. *Like that belated apology I still owe a friend.*

20
WEDNESDAY

"Therefore do not defile the land which you inhabit, in the midst of which I dwell. . . ."
—Numbers 35:34 (NKJV)

21
THURSDAY

"And the Lord shall guide thee continually. . . ." —Isaiah 58:11 (KJV)

22
FRIDAY
EARTH DAY

And let them have dominion . . . over all the earth and over every creeping thing that creeps on the earth. —Genesis 1:26 (ESV)

23
SATURDAY
PASSOVER

Cast thy burden upon Jehovah, and he will sustain thee. . . . —Psalm 55:22 (ASV)

Tidying the church had made me aware of the clutter that had accumulated in my own inner sanctum. It was time to ask God's forgiveness for becoming a spiritual litterbug.

—*Alma Barkman*

PRAYER REQUESTS _____

_____

_____

_____

APRIL

S	M	T	W	T	F	S
					1	2
3	4	5	6	7	8	9
10	11	12	13	14	15	16
17	18	19	20	21	22	23
24	25	26	27	28	29	30

OUR PRAYER

Father, help me to see Jesus just ahead,
even when the road is dark.

24
SUNDAY

Let what you heard from the beginning abide in you. If what you heard from the beginning abides in you, then you will abide in the Son and in the Father. —1 John 2:24 (NRSV)

25
MONDAY

"Ask, and it shall be given you; seek, and ye shall find; knock, and it shall be opened unto you." —Matthew 7:7 (KJV)

26
TUESDAY

Your statutes have been my songs in the house of my sojourning. I remember your name in the night, O Lord, and keep your law. —Psalm 119:54–55 (ESV)

FOR MOST OF MY LIFE, I've had a love relationship with picket fences. I've nearly had wrecks while driving, looking at them instead of the road. I've knocked on strangers' doors and asked to visit with their fences. When my husband, Gene, asked me what I wanted for my birthday, "A picket fence!" was my reply. I didn't want an entire fence. Our yard is much too large. I wanted just a piece of a picket fence.

"What will the fence *do*?" my husband asked.

"It won't *do* anything. It will just be," I answered. Gene didn't understand, but he commissioned a young man to build it anyway.

My heart thumped joyfully and tears stung my eyes when it was built. I ran to the fence, wishing I could throw my arms around it, but settled for touching it, stroking it, smiling at it, talking to it.

27
WEDNESDAY

"And God saw. . . ." —Genesis 1:31 (KJV)

28
THURSDAY

But the . . . Holy Ghost . . . he shall teach you all things, and bring all things to your remembrance. . . . —John 14:26 (KJV)

29
FRIDAY

And I will surely hide my face in that day on account of all the evil which they have done. . . . —Deuteronomy 31:18 (RSV)

30
SATURDAY

Don't worry about anything; instead, pray about everything. Tell God what you need, and thank him for all he has done. —Philippians 4:6 (NLT)

Gene stood at a distance, watching. "I'm glad you like it!" he called out. "It's okay that it doesn't do anything. It is nice."

Picket fences. No, Gene doesn't understand, but he loves me. And from his gift, I can learn daily the lesson of love. —*Marion Bond West*

PRAYER REQUESTS _____

_____

_____

_____

APRIL

S	M	T	W	T	F	S
					1	2
3	4	5	6	7	8	9
10	11	12	13	14	15	16
17	18	19	20	21	22	23
24	25	26	27	28	29	30

A PRAYER FOR MAY

Lord, purge our eyes to see
Within the seed a tree,
Within the glowing egg a bird,
Within the shroud a butterfly:
Till taught by such, we see
Beyond all creatures Thee,
And hearken for Thy tender word,
And hear it, "Fear not: it is I."

CHRISTINA ROSSETTI (1830–1894)

THE FIFTH COMMANDMENT

Age. Youth. Maturity. Age. Youth. Maturity.

This is the way the world goes round:
In tender continuity,
Generation after generation
Caring for the other,
Age for youth, maturity for age,
Each in its time.

Youth. Maturity. Age.
This is the way the world goes round:
We, God's grateful children
Held together by an endless chain,
Linked with love,
Honor bound.

❧ MAY 2016 ❧

SUNDAY	MONDAY	TUESDAY	WEDNESDAY	THURSDAY	FRIDAY	SATURDAY
1	2	3	4	5	6	7
8 MOTHER'S DAY	9	10	11	12	13	14
15 PENTECOST	16	17	18	19	20	21
22	23	24	25	26	27	28
29	30 MEMORIAL DAY	31				

NOTES

APRIL

S	M	T	W	T	F	S
					1	2
3	4	5	6	7	8	9
10	11	12	13	14	15	16
17	18	19	20	21	22	23
24	25	26	27	28	29	30

JUNE

S	M	T	W	T	F	S
			1	2	3	4
5	6	7	8	9	10	11
12	13	14	15	16	17	18
19	20	21	22	23	24	25
26	27	28	29	30		

OUR PRAYER

Thank You, Lord, for the gift of healing and the treasure of You.

1
SUNDAY

Kind words are like honey—sweet to the soul and healthy for the body.
—Proverbs 16:24 (NLT)

2
MONDAY

They are to do good, to be rich in good works, generous, and ready to share, thus storing up for themselves the treasure of a good foundation for the future, so that they may take hold of the life that really is life. —1 Timothy 6:18–19 (NRSV)

3
TUESDAY

"Open your homes to each other without complaining." —1 Peter 4:9 (GNB)

AT A WORKSHOP of "The Inspired Life," Joel and Michelle Levey asked participants to share thoughts about where they go for inspiration. "Listening to music," one man said. "Looking into my dog's eyes," a woman added. "Taking a walk in the woods," another participant offered. Michelle said simply, "I look at the clouds."

Then she told us about growing up in the Bronx, where the world was mostly concrete and glimpses of nature were rare. "But I could lie on my bed and look out my window, and there was just a tiny little slit above the tall buildings and rooftops through which I could see a sliver of sky. I especially loved the clouds because, in my child's mind, that was where God was. So I'd lie on my bed and commune with God that way. And even now, when I want to be inspired, I step outside my front door and look up at the clouds. It never fails to connect me with that which is beyond me."

4
WEDNESDAY

Greet those workers in the Lord, Tryphaena and Tryphosa. Greet the beloved Persis, who has worked hard in the Lord. —Romans 16:12 (NRSV)

5
THURSDAY

For what I do is not the good I want to do. . . . —Romans 7:19 (NIV)

6
FRIDAY

Those who hope in the Lord will renew their strength. They will soar on wings like eagles; they will run and not grow weary, they will walk and not be faint. —Isaiah 40:31 (NIV)

7
SATURDAY

"Consider how the wild flowers grow. They do not labor or spin." —Luke 12:27 (NIV)

I didn't grow up in the inner city, but I've found that looking up at the sky tunes me in to God too. May 5 is Ascension Day. What an appropriate time to step outside and connect with God by gazing at the clouds!

—*Marilyn Morgan King*

PRAYER REQUESTS _____

_____

_____

_____

MAY

S	M	T	W	T	F	S
1	2	3	4	5	6	7
8	9	10	11	12	13	14
15	16	17	18	19	20	21
22	23	24	25	26	27	28
29	30	31				

8
SUNDAY

MOTHER'S
DAY

"Many women have done excellently, but you surpass them all." —Proverbs 31:29 (NRSV)

9
MONDAY

He who finds a wife finds what is good, gaining favor from the Lord. —Proverbs 18:22 (CEB)

10
TUESDAY

"Encourage him. . . ." —Deuteronomy 1:38 (KJV)

MY MOTHER ALWAYS LOVED LILACS. From the time I was old enough to save my pennies for her birthday, she always had lilacs on May 11.

Then, in her last year, after a long downhill period of suffering, her mind wandered; she didn't remember where she was or who I was. So when May 11 came around, I thought, *Why bother? She hasn't responded to anything for days now.*

But tradition prevailed, and I arrived at the hospital with a small spray of her beloved blossoms.

As I arranged them in the vase on the bedside table, standing with my back to Mom's bed, a voice came forth clearly from

11
WEDNESDAY

"By day the Lord went ahead of them in a pillar of cloud to guide them on their way. . . ." —Exodus 13:21 (NIV)

12
THURSDAY

Now the serpent was more crafty than any of the wild animals the Lord God had made. —Genesis 3:1 (NIV)

13
FRIDAY

God is love. —1 John 4:8 (KJV)

14
SATURDAY

Do not remember the sins of my youth, nor my transgressions; according to Your mercy remember me, for Your goodness' sake, O Lord. —Psalm 25:7 (NKJV)

behind me. "How lovely! It's my birthday. You didn't forget."

For that one brief moment, just two weeks before she died, Mom came back for one last visit.

—*Naomi Lawrence*

PRAYER REQUESTS _____

_____

_____

_____

MAY

S	M	T	W	T	F	S
1	2	3	4	5	6	7
8	9	10	11	12	13	14
15	16	17	18	19	20	21
22	23	24	25	26	27	28
29	30	31				

Lord, reveal to me the areas of my life that
so easily ensnare my time and energy,
and help me to break those habits. Amen.

15
SUNDAY

PENTECOST

God is spirit, and those who worship him must worship in spirit and truth. —John 4:24 (ESV)

16
MONDAY

For all who are led by the Spirit of God are children of God. —Romans 8:14 (NRSV)

17
TUESDAY

The heavens are yours, and yours also the earth; you founded the world and all that is in it. —Psalm 89:11 (NIV)

PAUL TASHIRO WAS BORN in Japan. At the age of twelve, he volunteered as a kamikaze pilot. Fortunately, World War II ended before he could take off on his one-way mission. When he returned to Tokyo he had no home, and food and jobs were scarce, so he joined a gang of young soldiers selling drugs to American GIs.

After three years of leading a gangster life, Paul was passing by a tent one night when a burly American pulled him in. "When I heard the minister say, 'God gave His only begotten Son for you,' I was so happy to hear that someone still loved me, I began to cry." Paul said. "I confessed everything to Jesus that night." Paul came to the United States and enrolled in college, eventually becoming the only Japanese-born minister in the country at that time.

One day at a church in Tennessee, the congregation was singing "How Great Thou Art," when a blind, one-armed man came hobbling down the aisle, weeping. The singing died down as the man said, "Brother Paul, if I had met you five years ago, I would have killed you. I lost my arm and my eye-

18
WEDNESDAY

But in the seventh year there shall be a sabbath of complete rest for the land, and a sabbath for the Lord: you shall not sow your field or prune your vineyard. You shall not reap. . . . —Leviticus 25:4-5 (NRSV)

19
THURSDAY

"Ask the animals, and they will teach you. . . ." —Job 12:7 (NIV)

20
FRIDAY

They promise them freedom, while they themselves are slaves of depravity— for "people are slaves to whatever has mastered them." —2 Peter 2:19 (NIV)

21
SATURDAY

Casting all your anxiety on Him, because He cares for you. —1 Peter 5:7 (NAS)

sight to a kamikaze pilot." The American veteran wrapped his arm around the Japanese minister and said, "I love you." As the two men embraced, the voice of the congregation rose again in song: "How great thou art! How great thou art!"

—Marilyn Morgan King

PRAYER REQUESTS _____

_____

_____

_____

MAY

S	M	T	W	T	F	S
1	2	3	4	5	6	7
8	9	10	11	12	13	14
15	16	17	18	19	20	21
22	23	24	25	26	27	28
29	30	31				

OUR PRAYER

My quest for beauty has led me to You, Lord. Thank You.

22 SUNDAY	I will cry to God Most High. . . ." —Psalm 57:2 (NAS)
23 MONDAY	My times are in Your hand; deliver me from the hand of my enemies and from those who persecute me. —Psalm 31:15 (NAS)
24 TUESDAY	Your adornment must not be merely external . . . but let it be the hidden person of the heart. . . . —1 Peter 3:3–4 (NAS)

BROWSING THROUGH my concordance, I made the startling discovery that in the whole Bible there is not one mention of cats. As a cat lover, that bewildered me.

If the people in biblical times didn't have cats, how did they get rid of mice in their houses? They had mice; the Bible mentions mice about thirty times. And dogs are in there too. Of course, not every animal is mentioned in the Bible, but we do know cats existed then because their worship by Egyptians has been chronicled in their early art. (That may be one reason they aren't mentioned.)

But let me tell you why I think cats were neglected. The Bible was written down by human beings directly inspired by God, and I think that when God told some ancient scribe, "And then I created cats," the scribe didn't like cats and didn't write it down!

The point of my frivolous conjecture is this: if we cat lovers don't think cats have been given their fair due in biblical history, what are we going to do about that scribe?

25
WEDNESDAY

And God of all comfort, who comforts us in all our affliction so that we will be able to comfort those who are in any affliction with the comfort with which we ourselves are comforted by God. —2 Corinthians 1:3–4 (NAS)

26
THURSDAY

"For God sees not as man sees, for man looks at the outward appearance, but the Lord looks at the heart." —1 Samuel 16:7 (NAS)

27
FRIDAY

"You are altogether beautiful . . . And there is no blemish in you."
—Song of Solomon 4:7 (NAS)

28
SATURDAY

Two are better than one, because they have a good return for their labor.
—Ecclesiastes 4:9 (NIV)

Jesus gives us the answer: forgive those who trespass against us. Okay...this time!

—Glenn Kittler

PRAYER REQUESTS _____

_____

_____

_____

MAY

S	M	T	W	T	F	S
1	2	3	4	5	6	7
8	9	10	11	12	13	14
15	16	17	18	19	20	21
22	23	24	25	26	27	28
29	30	31				

Thou shalt not kill. —EXODUS 20:13 (KJV)

A PRAYER FOR JUNE

O God of earth and altar,
Bow down and hear our cry;
Our earthly rulers falter,
Our people drift and die;
The walls of gold entomb us,
The swords of scorn divide,
Take not thy thunder from us,
But take away our pride.

G. K. CHESTERTON (1874–1936)

THE SIXTH COMMANDMENT

When I was young, I fashioned
A slingshot from a maple fork
And a slice of inner tube.
My first shot
Was an idle one
Aimed at a catbird.
Astonishingly, the bird toppled from its perch
Dead.
Stunned, I tiptoed to it.
Caught in the unseeing glare of its
Yellow-black eye, I wept.
And, oh, God,
A dark corner of my heart has mourned
Ever since.
More lately I've been wondering
What other things I've killed,
Not meaning to, along the way.
By withholding an encouraging word,
How much enthusiasm
Have I killed, God?
By being a spoilsport,
How much joy?
By condemning,
How many reputations?
Yes, God, I am grown now,
And I've learned to love life more.
And loving life
Means helping all living things
And all things living
In hearts and minds
To flourish and grow.

JUNE 2016

SUNDAY	MONDAY	TUESDAY	WEDNESDAY	THURSDAY	FRIDAY	SATURDAY
			1	2	3	4
5	6	7	8	9	10	11
12	13	14 FLAG DAY	15	16	17	18
19 FATHER'S DAY	20 SUMMER BE-GINS	21	22	23	24	25
26	27	28	29	30		

NOTES

MAY

S	M	T	W	T	F	S
1	2	3	4	5	6	7
8	9	10	11	12	13	14
15	16	17	18	19	20	21
22	23	24	25	26	27	28
29	30	31				

JULY

S	M	T	W	T	F	S
					1	2
3	4	5	6	7	8	9
10	11	12	13	14	15	16
17	18	19	20	21	22	23
24/31	25	26	27	28	29	30

Today I will look with Your eyes, God,
seeing Your provision in all that I have.

29
SUNDAY

Bear one another's burdens, and so fulfill the law of Christ. —Galatians 6:2 (ESV)

30
MONDAY

MEMORIAL
DAY

"He being dead still speaks." —Hebrews 11:4 (NKJV)

31
TUESDAY

In the morning, Lord, you hear my voice; in the morning I lay my requests before you and wait expectantly. —Psalm 5:3 (NIV)

ALTHOUGH I'VE NEVER SERVED in the military, like most of my generation I was deeply affected by the Vietnam War. Many of us lost our political innocence and most of us, including me, lost friends. So the Vietnam Veterans Memorial holds a special place in my heart. I visited it that first year in 1982, and I've returned every year since.

A slash in the earth opens to receive the two arms of a wall that rise to meet in the middle and inspire reflection and healing. On the wall are carved the names of 58,286 men and women who died or remain missing in Vietnam. The wall has inspired people to leave offerings of love and forgiveness at its base. Medals, helmets, dog tags, and bracelets are accompanied by countless photographs and letters. Each night park rangers collect and preserve the offerings that have become a record of love and healing.

As the years passed, I wondered how long people would continue to leave things at the me-

JUNE | A man's heart plans his way, but the Lord directs his steps. —Proverbs 16:9 (NKJV)

1
WEDNESDAY

2
THURSDAY

"Let them rise up to your help, and let them be a shield unto you!"
—Deuteronomy 32:38 (JPS)

3
FRIDAY

"For everyone who asks receives, and everyone who searches finds, and for everyone who knocks, the door will be opened." —Luke 11:10 (NRSV)

4
SATURDAY

But I trust in your unfailing love. . . . —Psalm 13:5 (NIV)

morial. One day, I watched a pregnant woman leave a sonogram photo at the wall. "He would have been her grandfather," she said to her companion. Then I knew: the remembering would last for generations.

—Eric Fellman

PRAYER REQUESTS _____

_____

_____

_____

JUNE

S	M	T	W	T	F	S
			1	2	3	4
5	6	7	8	9	10	11
12	13	14	15	16	17	18
19	20	21	22	23	24	25
26	27	28	29	30		

Father, You are as near as my breath.
As long as I remember this, nothing can keep me from You.

5
SUNDAY

And who is a rock, except our God, The God who girds me with strength And makes my way blameless? —Psalm 18:31–32 (NAS)

6
MONDAY

In all thy ways acknowledge him, and he shall direct thy paths. —Proverbs 3:6 (KJV)

7
TUESDAY

Sovereign Lord, you are God! Your covenant is trustworthy, and you have promised these good things to your servant. —2 Samuel 7:28 (NIV)

SOMETIMES, WHEN LIFE GETS ROUGH, I need a towline to keep me from sinking. Over the years, certain Bible passages have been towlines that have held me up in turbulent waters. Here are a few with strong fibers I can hold on to when:

I'm tired. "I wait on the Lord to renew my strength" (Isaiah 40:31).

I am lonely. "God will never leave me, nor forsake me" (Hebrews 13:5).

I have financial worries. "My God shall supply all my need" (Philippians 4:19).

I'm depressed. "The Lord my God will enlighten my darkness" (Psalm 18:28).

I'm tempted. "God will not let me be tempted beyond my strength" (I Corinthians 10:13).

I'm feeling guilty. "Renew a right spirit within me" (Psalm 51:10).

I'm tense. "Peace I leave with you" (John 14:27).

Someone has wronged me. "If God be for me, who can be against?" (Romans 8:31).

I have too much to do. "God performs that which is appointed for me" (Job 23:14).

8
WEDNESDAY

When I was at the end of my rope, he saved me. —Psalm 116:6 (MSG)

9
THURSDAY

"My presence shall go with thee. . . ." —Exodus 33:14 (KJV)

10
FRIDAY

"How often I have wanted to gather your children together as a hen gathers her chicks beneath her wings, but you wouldn't let me." —Matthew 23:37 (TLB)

11
SATURDAY

"First the blade, then the ear, after that the full corn in the ear." —Mark 4:28 (KJV)

Maybe you'd like to add your favorite towlines to the list and keep them handy for those times when the sea of your life gets rough.

—*Marilyn Morgan King*

PRAYER REQUESTS _____

_____

_____

_____

JUNE

S	M	T	W	T	F	S
			1	2	3	4
5	6	7	8	9	10	11
12	13	14	15	16	17	18
19	20	21	22	23	24	25
26	27	28	29	30		

OUR PRAYER

Lord, let me be the answer when You call.

12
SUNDAY

O wretched man that I am! who shall deliver me from the body of this death?
—Romans 7:24 (KJV)

13
MONDAY

Uphold me according unto thy word, that I may live: and let me not be ashamed of my hope. —Psalm 119:116 (KJV)

14
TUESDAY

FLAG DAY

"Stand at the crossroads and look; ask for the ancient paths, ask where the good way is, and walk in it, and you will find rest for your souls. . . ." —Jeremiah 6:16 (NIV)

I WAS STRUGGLING WITH a particularly stubborn problem. I'd prayed about it feverishly for several weeks, begging, pleading, but without any results. Then one evening I walked outside to get the paper and found my son Paul, who was a toddler, trying to pull open the petals on a tightly closed rosebud. He looked up at me wide-eyed and said, "Paul make pretty flower bloom."

As I heard myself explaining to him that you can't make a flower bloom by pulling on it, something clicked inside of me. I had been handling my problem the way Paul had handled the rose. By begging, pleading, trying to force an answer, I had been trying to manipulate God. I needed to take my hands off, wait patiently, and trust in the creative power of God to open up a right answer for me. When the answer did come, it was not what I had expected. It was better. So my interference really had been blocking God's perfect solution to the problem.

15
WEDNESDAY

I will search for the lost. . . . —Ezekiel 34:16 (NIV)

16
THURSDAY

Bless the Lord, O my soul, And all that is within me, bless His holy name.
—Psalm 103:1 (NAS)

17
FRIDAY

Jesus replied, "They do not need to go away. You give them something to eat."
—Matthew 14:16 (NIV)

18
SATURDAY

Don't forget to be kind to strangers, for some who have done this have entertained angels without realizing it! —Hebrews 13:2 (TLB)

If you've been praying about something without results, maybe you need to take your hands off the problem, so God can make a perfect answer bloom.

—*Marilyn Morgan King*

PRAYER REQUESTS _____

_____

_____

_____

JUNE

S	M	T	W	T	F	S
			1	2	3	4
5	6	7	8	9	10	11
12	13	14	15	16	17	18
19	20	21	22	23	24	25
26	27	28	29	30		

*Father, please act in and through me even as
You give me rest from the work that You've blessed me with. Amen.*

19
SUNDAY

FATHER'S DAY

Honour thy father and thy mother, as the Lord thy God hath commanded thee. . . .
—Deuteronomy 5:16 (KJV)

20
MONDAY

SUMMER BEGINS

When they had finished eating, Jesus said to Simon Peter, "Simon son of John, do you love me more than these?" "Yes, Lord," he said, "you know that I love you." Jesus said, "Feed my lambs." —John 21:15 (NIV)

21
TUESDAY

Praise the Lord from the earth, you creatures of the ocean depths. Mountains and all hills, fruit trees and all cedars, wild animals and all livestock, small scurrying animals. . . .
—Psalm 148:7, 9–10 (NLT)

MY VAST IRISH-AMERICAN CLAN was at the dinner table on a bright summer evening, grandparents at either end and a gaggle of sons and daughters-in-law and mobs of children in between and a baby on a lap somewhere. Hilarity and hubbub were in the air.

"Pass the ketchup." "This is terrific pasta. Who made this pasta?" "Who's on the dishwashing crew?" "What time is the game tonight?"

A story started as my sister got up to get more food, and my brothers were laughing and correcting one another in loud voices getting louder. My dad, down at the end of the table where the king sits, cleared his throat and started to add to the story, but no one heard him. The conversation swirled on without him, and he subsided without being able to say his piece. I noticed this when it happened, but I said nothing.

Dad leaned back in his chair and didn't say anything for a while. I realized later that something

IT'S TIME TO ORDER YOUR COPY OF
GUIDEPOSTS DAILY PLANNER 2017!

3 EASY WAYS TO ORDER:

1. Order by mail. Return the coupon with payment.

2. Order by phone. Call (800) 932-2145.

3. Order online and **SAVE 10%**. Visit ShopGuideposts.org/DP2017. Use promo code DP2017.

✂ ···

(RETURN PORTION OF THIS FORM WITH YOUR PAYMENT.)

ORDER BY MAIL. Pay with check.

Yes! Send me *Guideposts Daily Planner 2017* for just $14.95 plus $3.99 shipping and processing.*

_____

Name (PLEASE PRINT)

_____

Address

_____

City   State   ZIP

Total copies ordered _____   Amount Enclosed $_____

14V74583DP

Method of Payment

*Connecticut/New York residents, please add sales tax.

Payment must accompany your order.

Please enclose your personal check or money order payable to Guideposts. No cash please.

Please allow 4 weeks for delivery.

Mail payment to:
Guideposts
PO Box 5822
Harlan, Iowa 51593

Guideposts

Guideposts

LOOKING FOR A GREAT GIFT IDEA?

Your search has ended! *Guideposts Daily Planner* makes a great gift that will be appreciated by everyone on your holiday list.

GUIDEPOSTS DAILY PLANNER
OFFERS YOU ALL OF THIS AND MORE!

- Organization at a glance
- Moving devotions to mark the passing months
- Hidden spiral binding, so your planner will lay flat
- A special place for prayer requests
- Encouraging Scripture verses to start each day

22
WEDNESDAY

If one member suffers, all suffer together; if one member is honored, all rejoice together. —1 Corinthians 12:26 (ESV)

23
THURSDAY

Enjoy the good of all his labour that he taketh under the sun all the days of his life, which God giveth him. . . . —Ecclesiastes 5:18 (KJV)

24
FRIDAY

"If you return to me and keep my commandments and do them, though your outcasts are under the farthest skies, I will gather them from there and bring them to the place at which I have chosen to establish my name." —Nehemiah 1:9 (NRSV)

25
SATURDAY

As for me, far be it from me that I should sin against the Lord by failing to pray for you. —1 Samuel 12:23 (NIV)

important in the family had passed at that moment, and that I wasn't brave enough to force the table to listen to the old king, and that I loved that man immensely for the king he had been—calm, generous, trustworthy, graceful.

—*Brian Doyle*

PRAYER REQUESTS _____

_____

_____

_____

JUNE

S	M	T	W	T	F	S
			1	2	3	4
5	6	7	8	9	10	11
12	13	14	15	16	17	18
19	20	21	22	23	24	25
26	27	28	29	30		

Lord, may I always say yes to invitations to adventure because with You, I can do more than I think I can.

26
SUNDAY

"He has risen from the dead. . . . Now I have told you." —Matthew 28:7 (NIV)

27
MONDAY

"Truly I tell you, anyone who will not receive the kingdom of God like a little child will never enter it." —Luke 18:17 (NIV)

28
TUESDAY

"God will let you laugh again. . . ." —Job 8:21 (MSG)

PANDA WAS MY FAVORITE TOY when I was five. That Christmas, the fire department collected old toys for poor children. Even though Panda begged me not to give him up, the voice of my Sunday school teacher quietly argued, "We never give God what we don't need. We give Him what we love the most."

Numb, I laid Panda on top of a pile of toys. I was heartbroken, but I didn't cry...then or for years. That would have meant I was selfish, and I didn't want to be selfish.

Ten years later I created a wonderful doll from my mother's scrap bag. I took McCall (I'd created her from a McCall's pattern) with me to my grandfather's beach house. I'm not sure when I took it into my head to give her away, or why, but by the time we reached the cabin I knew I would. And when we found the Pattersons, missionaries home on furlough, also at the beach, I knew I would give her to the youngest of the five girls.

"Are you sure you want to give away your doll?" my mother asked. This time I didn't hear my Sunday school teacher. I heard my own heart and

29
WEDNESDAY

This is the day which the Lord hath made; we will rejoice and be glad in it.
—Psalm 118:24 (KJV)

30
THURSDAY

Look to the Lord and his strength; seek his face always. —Psalm 105:4 (NIV)

JULY
1
FRIDAY

"Be strong and courageous. Do not be afraid . . . for the Lord your God goes with you. . . ."
—Deuteronomy 31:6 (NIV)

2
SATURDAY

Pray every way you know how, for everyone you know . . . . —1 Timothy 2:1 (MSG)

nodded. At fifteen I'd learned what my teacher hadn't understood: God didn't require me to give away my heart, just to give from my heart. I had made up my mind for myself, and so I could give gladly and freely.

—*Brenda Wilbee*

PRAYER REQUESTS _____

_____

_____

_____

JUNE

S	M	T	W	T	F	S
			1	2	3	4
5	6	7	8	9	10	11
12	13	14	15	16	17	18
19	20	21	22	23	24	25
26	27	28	29	30		

Thou shalt not commit adultery. —EXODUS 20:14 (KJV)

A PRAYER FOR JULY

O Lord,
help me not to despise
or oppose
what I do not
understand.

WILLIAM PENN (1644–1718)

THE SEVENTH COMMANDMENT

You meet quite by accident,
Two warm-hearted folks
Who know each other pleasantly.
It happens that your marriage partners are away.
You've always liked each other,
So why not plan to meet for dinner?
A quiet restaurant, the food's not bad…

But wait.

On second thought, better not.

Why not?

Because you risk too much.

Because emotions are too…well…
Too unpredictable.
Too easily ignited.
And if a spark should blaze up,
Who gets burned?

Everyone.

O God, help me to remember
The commitment I have made
To forsake all others
As long as I shall live.

And thank You for the peace
That Your commandment brings
To all who stop and heed it.

❧ JULY 2016 ❧

SUNDAY	MONDAY	TUESDAY	WEDNESDAY	THURSDAY	FRIDAY	SATURDAY
					1	2
3	4 INDEPENDENCE DAY	5	6	7	8	9
10	11	12	13	14	15	16
17	18	19	20	21	22	23
24 31	25	26	27	28	29	30

NOTES

JUNE

S	M	T	W	T	F	S
			1	2	3	4
5	6	7	8	9	10	11
12	13	14	15	16	17	18
19	20	21	22	23	24	25
26	27	28	29	30		

AUGUST

S	M	T	W	T	F	S
	1	2	3	4	5	6
7	8	9	10	11	12	13
14	15	16	17	18	19	20
21	22	23	24	25	26	27
28	29	30	31			

OUR PRAYER

Father, help me to keep my prayer life vibrant, interesting, and faithful.
Thank You for answering all prayers, no matter how they're said.

3
SUNDAY

"For you are standing on holy ground." —Exodus 3:5 (NLT)

4
MONDAY

INDEPENDENCE
DAY

I will lead the blind by ways they have not known, along unfamiliar paths I will guide them; I will turn the darkness into light before them and make the rough places smooth. . . . —Isaiah 42:16 (NIV)

5
TUESDAY

"I am the Lord your God, who brought you out of the land of Egypt, out of the house of bondage. You shall have no other gods before Me." —Exodus 20:2–3 (NKJV)

I WAS FIVE YEARS OLD when Grandfather taught me how to fold the American flag. It was the evening of the Fourth of July. A World War I veteran, he uncleated the flag and lowered it slowly into my waiting arms. We held it in our hands, and he snapped it like a sheet. Then we folded it, first lengthwise, and then end over end so that it formed a neat triangle with only the stars showing.

"Be careful," Grandfather warned. "Don't ever let it touch the ground. A flag will burn where it touches the ground."

For some time I thought the flag was made of some unique delicate fabric that would disintegrate when it touched the ground. When I saw old, frayed flags in museums, I often wondered if they were torn because they had touched the soil. When I saw the flag carried in parades, I held my breath, lest it hit the pavement. But as I grew older I realized that Grandfather was speaking metaphorically. He wanted me to respect the flag.

Keeping the flag off the ground might seem like a small thing, but it is in such gestures—

6
WEDNESDAY

"Keep these words that I am commanding you today in your heart."
—Deuteronomy 6:6 (NRSV)

7
THURSDAY

See to it that no one fail to obtain the grace of God; that no "root of bitterness" spring up and cause trouble. . . . —Hebrews 12:15 (RSV)

8
FRIDAY

Blessed be God, who didn't turn away when I was praying and didn't refuse me his kindness and love. —Psalm 66:20 (TLB)

9
SATURDAY

And whoever receives one such child in My name receives Me. —Matthew 18:5 (NAS)

that we show our care for our loved ones and our beloved country. For, as Grandfather knew, all those small gestures add up to prove where our hearts lie.

—*Rick Hamlin*

PRAYER REQUESTS _____

_____

_____

_____

JULY

S	M	T	W	T	F	S
					1	2
3	4	5	6	7	8	9
10	11	12	13	14	15	16
17	18	19	20	21	22	23
24/31	25	26	27	28	29	30

OUR PRAYER

It gets lonely down here, Lord.
Help me to be everyone's friend today.

10
SUNDAY

Long time therefore abode they speaking boldly in the Lord, which gave testimony unto the word of his grace. . . . —Acts 14:3 (KJV)

11
MONDAY

Do not be conformed to this world, but be transformed by the renewal of your mind. . . . —Romans 12:2 (ESV)

12
TUESDAY

Let all things be done decently and in order. —1 Corinthians 14:40 (KJV)

THE DAY FINALLY CAME when I had to have Suki put to sleep. Our Siamese cat had been sick a long time. She was thirteen years old.

"Nothing can be done," the veterinarian told me. "She's too old."

And so I took her to the animal hospital. *It's for the best,* I reassured myself. *She'll be out of her suffering.*

I signed the necessary papers. When it was over, I climbed into my car, slammed the door, and began to cry.

The next day I called a close friend. "I miss her," I said tearfully. "It's almost as though she were one of my children."

"Remember the good feeling we get during the holidays, listening to Christmas carols?" my friend asked gently. "Well, when something upsets me, I just put on Christmas music. The old, familiar songs always help."

At first I thought her suggestion strange. *Whoever heard of Christmas carols in July?* Still,

13
WEDNESDAY

I will declare your name to my brothers and sisters; I will praise you in the very center of the congregation! —Psalm 22:22 (CEB)

14
THURSDAY

Joseph her husband was a righteous man. —Matthew 1:19 (CEB)

15
FRIDAY

"At that moment Jesus' disciples returned, and they were greatly surprised to find him talking with a woman. . . ." —John 4:27 (TEV)

16
SATURDAY

O Lord, you are so good, so ready to forgive, so full of unfailing love for all who ask for your help. —Psalm 86:5 (NLT)

I decided to try it. As I sat listening to the words *Silent night, holy night, all is calm* I felt the pain lessen. Slowly, a sense of quiet filled me. "Sleep in heavenly peace, Suki," I prayed.

—Doris Haase

PRAYER REQUESTS _____

_____

_____

_____

JULY

S	M	T	W	T	F	S
					1	2
3	4	5	6	7	8	9
10	11	12	13	14	15	16
17	18	19	20	21	22	23
24/31	25	26	27	28	29	30

Lord, I have never been a patient person.
Help me remember that I live in Your time, come what may.

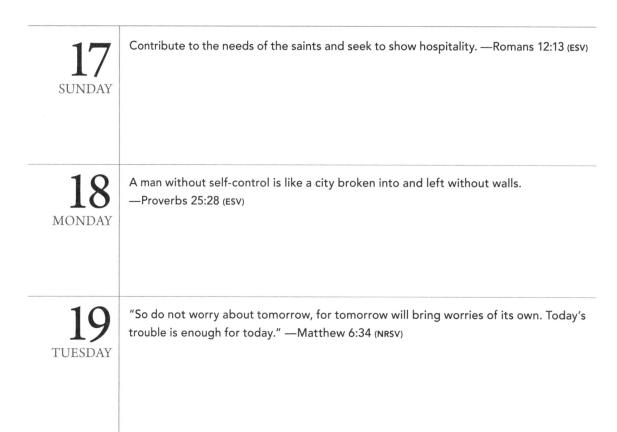

17
SUNDAY

Contribute to the needs of the saints and seek to show hospitality. —Romans 12:13 (ESV)

18
MONDAY

A man without self-control is like a city broken into and left without walls. —Proverbs 25:28 (ESV)

19
TUESDAY

"So do not worry about tomorrow, for tomorrow will bring worries of its own. Today's trouble is enough for today." —Matthew 6:34 (NRSV)

ONE SUMMER MORNING I took my Sunday school class of first- and second-graders to our church's spectacular flower garden. Tucked away behind the church, the garden has fragrant roses, marigolds, petunias, zinnias, nasturtium, and lavender.

"I want you to go into the garden with a partner and choose a flower. What is its shape? Is it tall or short? What is its smell? What does it remind you of? Then come back and we'll compare what you've found." My aim was to spark a wonder in them at the variety and beauty of God's creation.

The girls spread out into the flowers like butterflies, giggling and comparing. The boys, Turner and Gregory, got no farther than the grass. They plopped down and talked as if they were in a two-man huddle. Knowing their penchant for sports, I was sure that baseball—not flowers— was their topic.

I summoned the children to the picnic table. "I think we'll let Turner and Gregory go first," I said.

20
WEDNESDAY

Shout aloud and sing for joy, people of Zion, for great is the Holy One of Israel among you. —Isaiah 12:6 (NIV)

21
THURSDAY

And let the peace of Christ rule in your hearts, to which indeed you were called in one body. And be thankful. —Colossians 3:15 (ESV)

22
FRIDAY

But do not forget this one thing, dear friends: With the Lord a day is like a thousand years, and a thousand years are like a day. —2 Peter 3:8 (NIV)

23
SATURDAY

Purge me with hyssop, and I shall be clean; wash me, and I shall be whiter than snow. —Psalm 51:7 (NKJV)

"We picked a clover flower," Gregory said.

A clover? It never occurred to me to call such a lost-in-the-grass thing a flower.

"We thought it looked like a ballerina," Turner said.

"The wind is its music," added Gregory.

—*Shari Smyth*

PRAYER REQUESTS _____

_____

_____

_____

JULY

S	M	T	W	T	F	S
					1	2
3	4	5	6	7	8	9
10	11	12	13	14	15	16
17	18	19	20	21	22	23
24/31	25	26	27	28	29	30

OUR PRAYER
Lord, let us walk this labyrinth of life together.
Help me reflect Your light to all I meet.

24
SUNDAY

Yet you brought me out of the womb; you made me trust in you, even at my mother's breast. —Psalm 22:9 (NIV)

25
MONDAY

"And know. . . ." —Psalm 46:10 (KJV)

26
TUESDAY

Oh, the depth of the riches both of the wisdom and knowledge of God! How unsearchable are His judgments and unfathomable His ways! —Romans 11:33 (NAS)

JOHN HENRY TAKES wonderful care of our yard. He cuts the grass, weeds the flowerbeds, and plants shrubs. Sometimes when he's near our home, he stops by just to check on "his" yard. He tells my husband, Gene, marvelous hints such as, "You put out tomato plants with Epsom salts around the roots."

One day, I served John Henry lunch on the porch and went back inside. Suddenly, I heard this powerful voice, loudly calling, "God!" *Was John*

Henry hurt? I hurried outside and stopped in the doorway.

I had forgotten that he was deaf and sometimes speaks louder than is necessary. His prelunch blessing was loud enough for the entire neighborhood to hear. It wasn't a short, matter-of-fact blessing. It was a prayer by a man who was intimately acquainted with God. I bowed my head until it was finished. "And thank You for the food, for my good health, for my friends Gene

27
WEDNESDAY

Now faith is the substance of things hoped for, the evidence of things not seen.
—Hebrews 11:1 (KJV)

28
THURSDAY

He which testifieth these things saith, Surely I come quickly. Amen. Even so, come, Lord Jesus. —Revelation 22:20 (KJV)

29
FRIDAY

"And there will be no more night; they need no light of lamp or sun, for the Lord God will be their light . . . ." —Revelation 22:5 (NRSV)

30
SATURDAY

"The eyes of the Lord run to and fro throughout the whole earth . . . ."
—2 Chronicles 16:9 (KJV)

and Marion, and for the opportunity to care for our yard."

Back inside, I went to a chair where I like to pray and began to offer my thanks to the Lord... for John Henry and for "our" yard.

—*Marion Bond West*

PRAYER REQUESTS _____

_____

_____

_____

JULY

S	M	T	W	T	F	S
					1	2
3	4	5	6	7	8	9
10	11	12	13	14	15	16
17	18	19	20	21	22	23
24/31	25	26	27	28	29	30

Thou shalt not steal. —EXODUS 20:15 (KJV)

A PRAYER FOR AUGUST

Thou art never weary, O Lord,
of doing us good.
Let us never be weary
of doing Thee service.
But, as Thou hast pleasure in
the prosperity of Thy servants,
so let us take pleasure in
the service of our Lord,
and abound in·Thy work,
and in Thy love
and praise evermore.

JOHN WESLEY (1703–1791)

THE EIGHTH COMMANDMENT

Me steal, God?
Surely You don't mean me,
For I do believe I've never
consciously
taken property
unlawfully.

Office supplies?
Well, perhaps some little things
like that, but never many,
and anyway, that's common practice.
It's always seemed appropriate
for office supplies to be "appropriated."

Late?
Yes, I *was* late yesterday,
but that's hardly highway robbery.
No, I hadn't thought of
someone else's time as
something priceless gone to waste,
Never, ever, to be replaced.

Yes, God, yes,
I'm beginning now to see
the different things that I
can steal, unwittingly.
Teach me now,
before I go astray again;
that larceny's not just
black and white—
It also comes in gray.

❧ AUGUST 2016 ❧

SUNDAY	MONDAY	TUESDAY	WEDNESDAY	THURSDAY	FRIDAY	SATURDAY
	1	2	3	4	5	6
7	8	9	10	11	12	13
14	15	16	17	18	19	20
21	22	23	24	25	26	27
28	29	30	31			

NOTES

JULY

S	M	T	W	T	F	S
					1	2
3	4	5	6	7	8	9
10	11	12	13	14	15	16
17	18	19	20	21	22	23
24/31	25	26	27	28	29	30

SEPTEMBER

S	M	T	W	T	F	S
				1	2	3
4	5	6	7	8	9	10
11	12	13	14	15	16	17
18	19	20	21	22	23	24
25	26	27	28	29	30	

OUR PRAYER

Guide me, O God, in making the inspired words of Scripture my life's project, that I might bring Your hope to the world. Amen.

---

31 SUNDAY

Whatever your hand finds to do, do it with all your might . . . . —Ecclesiastes 9:10 (NIV)

AUGUST 1 MONDAY

He himself is before all things, and in him all things hold together. —Colossians 1:17 (NRSV)

---

2 TUESDAY

Great are the works of the Lord; they are pondered by all who delight in them. —Psalm 111:2 (NIV)

WHEN I WAS A KID growing up in Ohio, I made extra money picking strawberries for a man who had a small farm on the edge of town. He sold his produce from a little roadside stand. Because I was paid by the quart, I figured the faster I picked, the more I would make. But the farmer informed me that there was another requirement.

"Don't just fill your boxes to the edge. Fill them till they run over and won't hold any more," he said. "I've always operated on the principle that if I charge a fair price and give my customers a little extra, they'll come back again." And they did.

What I learned was that we reap what we sow… in every facet of our lives. Give the minimum, expect to receive the minimum. Give lavishly, extravagantly, and be rewarded in kind. Not that that should be our motivation. But the law that says you can't outgive the Lord is immutable. Jesus confirmed it when He preached, "Give and it will be given to you; good measure, pressed down, shaken

3
WEDNESDAY

The Lord opened her heart to respond to Paul's message. —Acts 16:14 (NIV)

4
THURSDAY

"But wisdom is proved right by her deeds." —Matthew 11:19 (NIV)

5
FRIDAY

But as for you . . . pursue righteousness, holy living, faithfulness, love, endurance, and gentleness. —1 Timothy 6:11 (CEB)

6
SATURDAY

"You shall teach them diligently to your children, and shall talk of them when you sit in your house, when you walk by the way, when you lie down, and when you rise up." —Deuteronomy 6:7 (NKJV)

together, running over, will be put into your lap. For the measure you give will be the measure you get back" (Luke 6:38, RSV).

It applies to strawberries—and the fruits of the Spirit, as well.

—*Fred Bauer*

PRAYER REQUESTS _____

_____

_____

_____

AUGUST

S	M	T	W	T	F	S
	1	2	3	4	5	6
7	8	9	10	11	12	13
14	15	16	17	18	19	20
21	22	23	24	25	26	27
28	29	30	31			

OUR PRAYER

Lord, help me always to accept Your will
even when things don't go as planned.

7
SUNDAY

"I have loved you with an everlasting love. . . ." —Jeremiah 31:3 (NIV)

8
MONDAY

Thou art my portion, O Lord: I have said that I would keep thy words. —Psalm 119:57 (KJV)

9
TUESDAY

"Come to me, all you that are weary and are carrying heavy burdens, and I will give you rest." —Matthew 11:28 (NRSV)

I READ A MAGAZINE article one day about an organization called the Not Terribly Good Club of Great Britain. It seems that a group of people who considered themselves failures in life decided to form the club for mutual moral support. In fact, some even took special pride in their negative status.

"Not many people have failed as completely as I!" one member is quoted as saying. The association was flourishing.

Then a Dutchman, Brother Andrew, joined them. After establishing his eligibility for membership, he explained that the real reason he wanted to belong was to be their chaplain. It was his desire to let all failures know that Jesus, Whose mission apparently failed when He died on the Cross, turned that defeat into the greatest victory of all time.

"There's no such thing as failure for Christians," Brother Andrew asserted. Unfortunately for

10
WEDNESDAY

And thine ears shall hear a word behind thee, saying, This is the way, walk ye in it . . . . —Isaiah 30:21 (KJV)

11
THURSDAY

Many are the plans in the mind of a man, but it is the purpose of the Lord that will stand. —Proverbs 19:21 (ESV)

12
FRIDAY

Husbands, go all out in your love for your wives. . . . —Ephesians 5:25 (MSG)

13
SATURDAY

Then make my joy complete by being like-minded, having the same love, being one in spirit and of one mind. —Philippians 2:2 (NIV)

the club, many believed him. In fact, I understand that following his statement, the membership fell off so drastically that the club no longer exists!

—Doris Haase

PRAYER REQUESTS _____

_____

_____

_____

AUGUST

S	M	T	W	T	F	S
	1	2	3	4	5	6
7	8	9	10	11	12	13
14	15	16	17	18	19	20
21	22	23	24	25	26	27
28	29	30	31			

OUR PRAYER

Precious Savior, I almost failed to forgive my friend.
Help me to never withhold what You've so freely given to me.

14
SUNDAY

Now I know in part; then I shall know fully, even as I am fully known.
—1 Corinthians 13:12 (NIV)

15
MONDAY

For the Lord is good; his steadfast love endures for ever, and his faithfulness to all generations. —Psalm 100:5 (ESV)

16
TUESDAY

The sabbath was made for man. . . . —Mark 2:27 (KJV)

WHEN I FIRST BEGAN wage-earning, I determined to finance a "real vacation" for my mother. So for many weeks I saved my extra dollars. At last, I proudly presented a full envelope to Mom. Her moist eyes and warm hug filled my heart.

One month later, when we sat down for dinner, I noticed that Mom looked more tired and drawn than ever. "When are you going to take that vacation?" I demanded.

At first, Mom didn't answer. But after much poking and prodding, she finally admitted that she had given the money to Daddy "because he had desperate need of it."

Mom heard my reproaches in silence for a time. Then she held up her hand and with a soft smile asked, "Whom did you give your gift to?"

"That's just it!" I exclaimed. "I gave it to you, not to Dad!"

"Rosie," she said, "when you give something, *really* give it away. If you had done this, you

17
WEDNESDAY

Be happy about it! Be very glad! For a tremendous reward awaits you up in heaven. —Matthew 5:12 (TLB)

18
THURSDAY

In every situation, by prayer and petition, with thanksgiving, present your requests to God. —Philippians 4:6 (NIV)

19
FRIDAY

"For if you forgive others for their transgressions, your heavenly Father will also forgive you." —Matthew 6:14 (NAS)

20
SATURDAY

The heart of man plans his way, but the Lord establishes his steps. —Proverbs 16:9 (ESV)

wouldn't be worrying now about how I used it."

How right she was! I've fretted about children spending *my* money on things they'll discard the next day. I've nagged my husband for not wearing *my* cufflinks. How foolish. How selfish.

—Rosalyn Hart Finch

PRAYER REQUESTS _____

_____

_____

_____

AUGUST

S	M	T	W	T	F	S
	1	2	3	4	5	6
7	8	9	10	11	12	13
14	15	16	17	18	19	20
21	22	23	24	25	26	27
28	29	30	31			

OUR PRAYER

Father, give me the wisdom of a child, smart enough to find
Your joy as I work beside You . . . even if it's hand-washing socks!

21
SUNDAY

The Pharisees watched him to see whether he would cure on the sabbath, so that they might find an accusation against him. . . . Jesus said . . . "Is it lawful to do good or to do harm on the sabbath, to save life or to destroy it?" —Luke 6:7, 9 (NRSV)

22
MONDAY

To them God has chosen to make known among the Gentiles the glorious riches of this mystery, which is Christ in you, the hope of glory. —Colossians 1:27 (NIV)

23
TUESDAY

Friends love you like a sister or brother—they are born to give support during adversity. —Proverbs 17:17 (TIB)

"WHAT'S THAT IN YOUR HAND?" the pastor asked in his sermon. His text was Exodus 4:2 on God's question to Moses, who held a staff in his hands. The pastor's message was about giving God whatever we hold in our hands because God uses what we offer to help us change and grow and to help others through our offerings.

The question reminded me of a game we often play with children. We put a piece of candy in one hand and nothing in the other and then offer both closed hands to the child, asking, "What's in my hand?" We push the candy hand out a little and pull the empty hand back, because we're eager to give the child the candy.

I play the same game with God. I eagerly offer what I want to give out of my fullness: the money for the church offering, or my free hour once a week, or the abilities I think of as my strengths. But what about the things in my "empty hand"? The weaknesses I'd rather hide or my fears or mistakes? They need to be offered to God as well.

24
WEDNESDAY

"No one can come to me unless the Father who sent me draws them, and I will raise them up at the last day." —John 6:44 (NIV)

25
THURSDAY

"When you pray, don't pour out a flood of empty words. . . ." —Matthew 6:7 (CEB)

26
FRIDAY

"Well done . . . enter thou into the joy of thy lord." —Matthew 25:21 (KJV)

27
SATURDAY

And offer every part of yourself to him [God] as an instrument of righteousness. —Romans 6:13 (NIV)

When the offering plate came by, I opened both hands, and along with my money, I gave some offerings out of my emptiness—my pride, my impatience, my struggle with quick criticism—with a prayer.

—*Carol Kuykendall*

PRAYER REQUESTS _____

_____

_____

_____

AUGUST

S	M	T	W	T	F	S
	1	2	3	4	5	6
7	8	9	10	11	12	13
14	15	16	17	18	19	20
21	22	23	24	25	26	27
28	29	30	31			

Lord, when I get caught up in the complexities of life,
remind me to recount Your great deeds. Amen.

28
SUNDAY

Honor the Lord with your wealth and with the best part of everything. . . .
—Proverbs 3:9 (NLT)

29
MONDAY

When the poor and needy seek water, and there is none, and their tongue faileth for thirst, I the Lord will hear them, I the God of Israel will not forsake them. I will open rivers in high places, and fountains in the midst of the valleys: I will make the wilderness a pool of water, and the dry land springs of water. —Isaiah 41:17–18 (KJV)

30
TUESDAY

So then, my beloved brethren, let every man be swift to hear, slow to speak, slow to wrath. —James 1:19 (NKJV)

YOU KNOW WHAT WE HAVE here in Arizona? Lizards! Dozens of them! They scramble beneath our bushes and skitter across our fence, stopping to sun themselves on the warm concrete. They're not beautiful or cuddly-looking, but they are fun to watch and they've taught me something.

When these resourceful little creatures are attacked, their tails break off, allowing them to escape. Some even have striped or brightly colored tails that entice their predators to attack this less vulnerable spot. Then the lizard immediately begins to grow a new tail and can go through this routine an unlimited number of times.

I wish I could let go as easily when I feel under attack. Recently, a friend jumped on me when I told her what I'd do if I were in her place. "I don't need a lecture!" she said. Her words stung. In retreat, I not only decided I didn't want to talk to her, but I also avoided being with her. She may have been wrong, but I held on to my anger way too

31
WEDNESDAY

And we know that in all things God works for the good of those who love him, who have been called according to his purpose. —Romans 8:28 (NIV)

SEPTEMBER
1
THURSDAY

Hope in the Lord! Be strong! Let your heart take courage! Hope in the Lord! —Psalm 27:14 (CEB)

2
FRIDAY

It is good to praise the Lord . . . proclaiming your love in the morning and your faithfulness at night. —Psalm 92:1–2 (NIV)

3
SATURDAY

"Out in the world the master sits at the table and is served by his servants. But not here! For I am your servant." —Luke 22:27 (TLB)

long, risking a fine friendship. It took some time, but we realized our mistakes and came together to mend the rift.

I've learned a simple lesson from the lizard: let it go. And let God's love heal the broken places like new.

—*Gina Bridgeman*

PRAYER REQUESTS _____

_____

_____

_____

AUGUST

S	M	T	W	T	F	S
	1	2	3	4	5	6
7	8	9	10	11	12	13
14	15	16	17	18	19	20
21	22	23	24	25	26	27
28	29	30	31			

Thou shalt not bear false witness against thy neighbor. —EXODUS 20:16 (KJV)

A PRAYER FOR SEPTEMBER

Jesus,
Master Carpenter of Nazareth,
Who on the cross
through wood and nails
didst work man's whole salvation:
Wield well Thy tools
in this Thy workshop;
that we who come
to Thee rough hewn
may by Thy hand
be fashioned to a truer beauty
and a greater usefulness,
for the honor of Thy name.

HAL PINK, BRITISH VETERAN OF WORLD WAR I

THE NINTH COMMANDMENT

One day in court
I placed my hand upon the Bible
And swore to tell the truth
The whole truth
So help me God.

Then I sat and proceeded to tell the court
Partial truths
Twisted truths
Anything to make my case look good.

And so it went
Closer and closer to outright lying
Until suddenly—this is hard to believe—
My hand began to hurt,
The same hand I'd rested on the Bible.

I knew what it was telling me.
It was saying: Don't ever say
To your neighbors
Words you'd never dare say to God.

Now I place my hand on Your Word
Once more, God.
Help me be a true witness.
Help me, please.

❧ SEPTEMBER 2016 ❧

SUNDAY	MONDAY	TUESDAY	WEDNESDAY	THURSDAY	FRIDAY	SATURDAY
				1	2	3
4	5 LABOR DAY	6	7	8	9	10
11	12	13	14	15	16	17
18	19	20	21	22 FALL BEGINS	23	24
25	26	27	28	29	30	

NOTES

AUGUST

S	M	T	W	T	F	S
	1	2	3	4	5	6
7	8	9	10	11	12	13
14	15	16	17	18	19	20
21	22	23	24	25	26	27
28	29	30	31			

OCTOBER

S	M	T	W	T	F	S
						1
2	3	4	5	6	7	8
9	10	11	12	13	14	15
16	17	18	19	20	21	22
23/30	24/31	25	26	27	28	29

Lord, You have shown me that the greatest charity happens when it is directed toward the least among us.

4
SUNDAY

In him the whole building is joined together and rises to become a holy temple in the Lord. And in him you too are being built together to become a dwelling in which God lives by his Spirit. —Ephesians 2:21–22 (NIV)

5
MONDAY

LABOR DAY

The sleep of a labouring man is sweet . . . . —Ecclesiastes 5:12 (KJV)

6
TUESDAY

Everything that lives and moves will be your food. —Genesis 9:3 (GW)

I HAD THOUGHT OF every excuse to fire Toby, my assistant in an advertising office. He was talented and efficient, but he and I were at constant odds, and colleagues told me that he had even tried to undermine me with my boss. Finally, to my immense relief, he resigned.

A few years later, the president of another company asked if I knew of a good person to head his advertising department. Though I tried to duck it, Toby's name came to mind. He filled the job description, but after what he and I had been through…

I held a little debate with myself. *Could he do the job? Yes, he's a natural. Well?*

The next day I called Toby, and the day after that he accepted the job. But it wasn't until he invited me to dinner that I fully realized that I had done the right thing. He confessed his former enmity and asked my forgiveness. As we shook hands, he said, "Friends are better than enemies, aren't they?"

7 WEDNESDAY

Blessed are you when men . . . utter all kinds of evil against you falsely . . . .
—Matthew 5:11 (RSV)

8 THURSDAY

My God will fully satisfy every need of yours according to his riches in glory in Christ Jesus. —Philippians 4:19 (NRSV)

9 FRIDAY

The Lord is good to all, and His tender mercies are over all His works. —Psalm 145:9 (NKJV)

10 SATURDAY

Therefore encourage one another and build each other up, just as in fact you are doing. —1 Thessalonians 5:11 (NIV)

It was then that the truth of the biblical instruction "Love your enemies" came surging through. When you love them, they perform a wonderful vanishing act and return as friends.

—*Charles M. Davis*

PRAYER REQUESTS _____

_____

_____

_____

SEPTEMBER

S	M	T	W	T	F	S
				1	2	3
4	5	6	7	8	9	10
11	12	13	14	15	16	17
18	19	20	21	22	23	24
25	26	27	28	29	30	

OUR PRAYER

Father, help me keep my eyes open and reach out
to help those who are right under my nose.

11
SUNDAY

Worship the Lord with gladness. . . . —Psalm 100:2 (NIV)

12
MONDAY

. . . So that you may stand mature and fully assured in everything that God wills.
—Colossians 4:12 (NRSV)

13
TUESDAY

On the day the Lord gave the Amorites into the power of Israel, Joshua spoke to the
Lord . . . "Sun, stand still at Gibeon! and Moon, at the Aijalon Valley!" The sun stood
still and the moon stood motionless until a nation took revenge on its enemies.
—Joshua 10:12–13 (CEB)

THE DAY WAS SUNNY and mellow and smelling of changing birch leaves. I took my grandchildren Zachary and Hannah to play in the park. Soon an older woman meandered by with a young child in tow. She nodded and smiled, but didn't seem inclined to chat. Her little charge toddled off across the grass with Hannah.

Zachary and I teeter-tottered while the girls sailed down a small slide beneath the watchful eye of the unknown woman. When I twirled my grandchildren on the tire swing, the other child wanted to swing too, and the woman came over to help. Haltingly, she told me she was from Russia, visiting her daughter and granddaughter.

"Oh," I exclaimed, "you're a *babushka*!" She laughed, nodding. I pointed to myself. "Me too," I said.

Here we were, two grandmothers from countries that used to be enemies, playing in the park with our grandchildren, teaching them to get along, and watching out for them with equal concern.

The two of us left the park, taking our grand-

14
WEDNESDAY

This is the message we have heard from him and declare to you: God is light; in him there is no darkness at all. —1 John 1:5 (NIV)

15
THURSDAY

As for God, his way is perfect: The Lord's word is flawless; he shields all who take refuge in him. —Psalm 18:30 (NIV)

16
FRIDAY

"You must love and help your neighbors just as much as you love and take care of yourself." —James 2:8 (TLB)

17
SATURDAY

For by him were all things created, that are in heaven, and that are in earth, visible and invisible, whether they be thrones, or dominions, or principalities, or powers: all things were created by him, and for him. —Colossians 1:16 (KJV)

children in opposite directions. We had met only briefly, but it was long enough for me to gain new understanding of a grandmother's mission: to help shape our world's future by sowing seeds of consideration and respect...starting in the park.

—*Carol Knapp*

PRAYER REQUESTS _____

_____

_____

_____

SEPTEMBER

S	M	T	W	T	F	S
				1	2	3
4	5	6	7	8	9	10
11	12	13	14	15	16	17
18	19	20	21	22	23	24
25	26	27	28	29	30	

OUR PRAYER

Dear Father, You smile when Your children enjoy life.
Help me to see every day as a blessing from You. Amen

18
SUNDAY

Praise God in his sanctuary . . . . —Psalm 150:1 (NIV)

19
MONDAY

Anxiety weighs down the heart. —Proverbs 12:25 (NIV)

20
TUESDAY

"But I say to you that if you are angry with a brother or sister, you will be liable to judgment; and if you insult a brother or sister, you will be liable to the council. . . ."
—Matthew 5:22 (NRSV)

OUR FRIEND RICHARD is a pleasant, down-to-earth guy, and when he moved to a new community he decided to look for a church where he could become part of the family. He was intrigued when he read that one of the local churches was celebrating its sixtieth anniversary, and as part of the festivities, everyone was invited to come on Sunday morning dressed in the fashion of the 1930s.

"This sounded like my idea of an interesting place, so I showed up in what I knew people would have worn then: bib overalls, work boots, and a red bandanna. I was early, so I went in and sat down. The first man I saw wasn't dressed properly for the celebration, but I decided he must be an usher. Then a woman came in, wearing regular Sunday clothes. *She has to sing in the choir,* I thought.

"The pews began to fill up and, slowly, the realization dawned on me that nobody else was in costume. I was in the wrong church! I stayed for the service, but no one sat near me and not one person greeted me. Beautiful building, good sermon, nice music, but I never went back."

21
WEDNESDAY

"Jesus . . . who went about doing good . . . ." —Acts 10:38 (NKJV)

22
THURSDAY

FALL BEGINS

Even though I walk through the darkest valley, I fear no evil; for you are with me; your rod and your staff —they comfort me. —Psalm 23:4 (NRSV)

23
FRIDAY

"Do not store up for yourselves treasures on earth, where moths and vermin consume, and where thieves break in and steal. But store up for yourselves treasures in heaven. . . ." —Matthew 6:19–20 (NIV)

24
SATURDAY

He satisfies the longing soul. . . . —Psalm 107:9 (NKJV)

When Richard told us that story, I couldn't help imagining myself as a member of that congregation. *If I had been there, how would I have responded to this visitor?*

—*Mary Jane Clark*

PRAYER REQUESTS _____

_____

_____

_____

SEPTEMBER

S	M	T	W	T	F	S
				1	2	3
4	5	6	7	8	9	10
11	12	13	14	15	16	17
18	19	20	21	22	23	24
25	26	27	28	29	30	

OUR PRAYER

Thank You, Lord, for the kindness of strangers.

25
SUNDAY

Then Jesus said unto them . . . Walk while ye have the light, lest darkness come upon you: for he that walketh in darkness knoweth not whither he goeth. —John 12:35 (KJV)

26
MONDAY

"For even the Son of Man came not to be served but to serve. . . ." —Mark 10:45 (ESV)

27
TUESDAY

For when I am weak, then I am strong. —2 Corinthians 12:10 (NIV)

"OH NO!" I MOANED out loud, spotting my son's math homework on the kitchen counter. More than once I had reminded Derek to put the papers in his school bag so he wouldn't forget them, and obviously he hadn't obeyed me.

What shall I do? I wondered. Actually, I knew what I was supposed to do. Nothing. According to all the parenting books, parents are not supposed to assume responsibility for their children's mistakes. They are supposed to let them learn from their mistakes by allowing them to suffer the natural consequences of their actions. I ached thinking of the embarrassment and disappointment my son would feel when he discovered he didn't have his homework, and I had to talk myself out of driving to school.

I shared my feelings with a friend who said, "I faced the same problem one day last week, but I took Jana's homework to her and used it as an opportunity to teach her the meaning of grace. She knew she didn't deserve the delivery service, but I did it simply because I love her. God does the same for us all the time."

28
WEDNESDAY

It is written: " 'As surely as I live,' says the Lord, 'every knee will bow before me; every tongue will acknowledge God.' " —Romans 14:11 (NIV)

29
THURSDAY

God said, "Let there be light" . . . . —Genesis 1:3 (JPS)

30
FRIDAY

"I was a stranger and you welcomed me." —Matthew 25:35 (NRSV)

OCTOBER

1
SATURDAY

I am small and despised, yet I do not forget thy precepts. —Psalm 119:141 (RSV)

It was too late for me to deliver the math papers to school, but I knew I'd have another chance. I look forward to sharing the lesson I just learned about grace.

—Carol Kuykendall

PRAYER REQUESTS _____

_____

_____

_____

SEPTEMBER

S	M	T	W	T	F	S
				1	2	3
4	5	6	7	8	9	10
11	12	13	14	15	16	17
18	19	20	21	22	23	24
25	26	27	28	29	30	

Thou shalt not covet.... —EXODUS 20:17 (KJV)

A PRAYER FOR OCTOBER

Lord,
I know not what I ought
to ask of Thee;
Thou only knowest what I need;
Thou lovest me better
than I know how to love myself.
O Father,
give to Thy child that which.
he knows not how to ask.

FRANCIS FÉNELON (1651–1715)

THE TENTH COMMANDMENT

My neighbors had all the goods.
A fine house, fancy car, blue-chip stocks
And an inheritance in the offing.
Aha! But they sold their soul—
In the reaping, no?
No. They were gentle, kind, and generous.

I should've felt lucky to have friends
Whom fortune had smiled so sweetly on.
Should've given thanks for friends
Who shared so fully—but I didn't.
Didn't give one single
Thing in return.
Because I was poor—wretchedly so
In the spite-filled way those who
Covet always are.

And so the day came, of course it came,
When I couldn't bear their riches
Any more. And so I hid,
Hid in my painful envy.
But then, one lonely afternoon,
There they were again, at my door,
Offering me a gift I hadn't earned.
Offering me the one thing I hadn't coveted:
Their friendship. Their greatest wealth.

That day I, too, became rich,
For at last I'd come to know
That there are things
More valuable than things.

❧ OCTOBER 2016 ❧

SUNDAY	MONDAY	TUESDAY	WEDNESDAY	THURSDAY	FRIDAY	SATURDAY
						1
2	3 ROSH HASHANAH	4	5	6	7	8
9	10	11	12 YOM KIPPUR	13	14	15
16	17	18	19	20	21	22
23 / 30	24 UNITED NATIONS DAY / HALLOWEEN 31	25	26	27	28	29

NOTES

SEPTEMBER

S	M	T	W	T	F	S
				1	2	3
4	5	6	7	8	9	10
11	12	13	14	15	16	17
18	19	20	21	22	23	24
25	26	27	28	29	30	

NOVEMBER

S	M	T	W	T	F	S
		1	2	3	4	5
6	7	8	9	10	11	12
13	14	15	16	17	18	19
20	21	22	23	24	25	26
27	28	29	30			

OUR PRAYER

Lord Jesus, there will always be highs and lows in life. Thank You for helping me understand that the difference between them is often my attitude.

2
SUNDAY

Exercise yourself spiritually, and practice being a better Christian because that will help you not only now in this life, but in the next life too. —1 Timothy 4:8 (TLB)

3
MONDAY

ROSH HASHANAH

The patient in spirit is better than the proud in spirit. —Ecclesiastes 7:8 (RSV)

4
TUESDAY

Taste and see that the Lord is good; blessed is the one who takes refuge in him. —Psalm 34:8 (NIV)

WHEN MY YOUNGEST SON, JOHN, was a toddler, he became separated from me in a large store. I went from department to department, asking the clerks if they'd seen a little boy in a green and yellow Big Bird shirt. Time and again, they answered, "He was here a few minutes ago, calling for his mommy, but he rushed away before we could help him find you." When we finally connected, we agreed that if we ever got separated again, he'd stay right where he was and wait for me to find him.

That's what we need to do when we're feeling separated from God. We all have times when our prayers seem to bounce off invisible walls; times when, no matter what we do, we can't seem to feel the presence of God. It's a cold, dark feeling that often makes us

5
WEDNESDAY

Give generously to them and do so without a grudging heart. . . .
—Deuteronomy 15:10 (NIV)

6
THURSDAY

Every perfect gift is from above, and comes down from the Father of lights. . . .
—James 1:17 (NKJV)

7
FRIDAY

No matter what happens, always be thankful, for this is God's will for you who belong to Christ Jesus. —1 Thessalonians 5:18 (TLB)

8
SATURDAY

But the Comforter, which is the Holy Ghost, whom the Father will send in my name, he shall . . . bring all things to your remembrance. . . . —John 14:26 (KJV)

either pray more frantically and ineffectively or turn farther away. What we really need to do is go within, still our clanging thoughts, and wait for God to draw us gently back.

—*Marilyn Morgan King*

PRAYER REQUESTS _____

_____

_____

_____

OCTOBER

S	M	T	W	T	F	S
						1
2	3	4	5	6	7	8
9	10	11	12	13	14	15
16	17	18	19	20	21	22
23/30	24/31	25	26	27	28	29

9
SUNDAY

"Abigail . . . was a woman of good understanding and a beautiful appearance. . . ."
—1 Samuel 25:3 (NKJV)

10
MONDAY

He will cover you with his feathers, and under his wings you will find refuge. . . .
—Psalm 91:4 (NIV)

11
TUESDAY

"You are a good and faithful servant! You've been faithful over a little. I'll put you in charge of much. Come, celebrate with me." —Matthew 25:21 (CEB)

I PARKED IN FRONT of Judy's office building, dreading my weekly appointment. This was my fourth month of therapy, but something in me still fought the idea of revealing myself to a counselor, even though I knew she would not judge me. Closing my eyes for a moment, I recalled a sign I'd seen in front of a church: In the Stress of the Storm, Learn the Strength of the Anchor.

Ninety minutes later, I walked back to the parking lot, relieved that another session was behind me, yet grateful for my capable thera-pist. Today we had discussed my need to have the stools in my kitchen aligned precisely with each other and the place mats on the table positioned squarely with the chairs in front of them. It was the same with the pillows on the sofa and the books on the shelf. My world had to be symmetrical.

Judy was able to put a name to my problem: obsessive-compulsive personality, which is a less severe form of obsessive-compulsive disorder. Both impairments are anxiety-related and can be

12
WEDNESDAY

YOM KIPPUR

You know when I sit down and when I rise up; you discern my thoughts from far away. You search out my path and my lying down, and are acquainted with all my ways. —Psalm 139:2–3 (NRSV)

13
THURSDAY

He explores the mountains for his pasture and searches after every green thing. —Job 39:8 (NAS)

14
FRIDAY

Where can I go from your Spirit? Where can I flee from your presence? If I go up to the heavens, you are there; if I make my bed in the depths, you are there. —Psalm 139:7–8 (NIV)

15
SATURDAY

Even to your old age I am he, and to gray hairs I will carry you. I have made, and I will bear; I will carry and will save. —Isaiah 46:4 (ESV)

treated successfully with medication. How freeing finally to have that knowledge!

There would be more to learn on my path of self-discovery, but the Perfect One was my anchor and I was finding that sufficient indeed.

—*Libbie Adams*

PRAYER REQUESTS _____

_____

_____

_____

OCTOBER

S	M	T	W	T	F	S
						1
2	3	4	5	6	7	8
9	10	11	12	13	14	15
16	17	18	19	20	21	22
23/30	24/31	25	26	27	28	29

OUR PRAYER

How delightful songs are, Lord!
Surely we inherited the urge to sing from You.

16
SUNDAY

"See, I am sending an angel ahead of you to guard you along the way and to bring you to the place I have prepared." —Exodus 23:20 (NIV)

17
MONDAY

But if a woman has long hair, it is her glory? . . . —1 Corinthians 11:15 (NRSV)

18
TUESDAY

He said, "Go away; for the girl is not dead but sleeping." And they laughed at him. . . . He went in and took her by the hand, and the girl got up. —Matthew 9:24–25 (NRSV)

A STORM SOME TIME BACK caused severe flooding and extensive damage to property in the South. Several bridges were wiped out along one river, and traffic had to be detoured many miles upstream. A group of hikers was stranded. Wet and cold, they began to worry about where they were going to spend the night. Then they came upon a big wooden cross that had been blown into the water from a campground. It offered a way to reach the other side. On their hands and knees, the hikers used the cross to crawl over the swirling waters.

This is not the first time a cross has served to rescue stranded souls. Songwriter Ralph E. Hudson described his salvation experience in the chorus that he added to Isaac Watts's hymn "Alas, and Did My Savior Bleed?"

At the cross, at the cross,
    where I first saw the light
And the burden of my heart rolled away,
It was there by faith I received my sight,
And now I am happy all the day.

19
WEDNESDAY

But God has surely listened and has heard my prayer. —Psalm 66:19 (NIV)

20
THURSDAY

"Blessed is she who has believed that the Lord would fulfill to her his promises!"
—Luke 1:45 (NIV)

21
FRIDAY

"Sing to the Lord a new song. . . ." —Psalm 149:1 (NIV)

22
SATURDAY

Contribute to the needs of God's people, and welcome strangers into your home.
—Romans 12:13 (CEB)

Whenever our journey is interrupted by storms, whenever our pathway is blocked by difficulties, whenever we face obstacles that are impossible to scale alone, we can find help at the foot of the Cross. Jesus is always our bridge over troubled waters.

—*Fred Bauer*

PRAYER REQUESTS _____

_____

_____

_____

OCTOBER

S	M	T	W	T	F	S
						1
2	3	4	5	6	7	8
9	10	11	12	13	14	15
16	17	18	19	20	21	22
23/30	24/31	25	26	27	28	29

OUR PRAYER

Lord, it's Your grace that's brought me safe thus far;
may that same grace lead me home.

23
SUNDAY

If any of you lacks wisdom, you should ask God . . . and it will be given to you.
—James 1:5–6 (NIV)

24
MONDAY

UNITED
NATIONS DAY

The wilderness and the wasteland shall be glad for them, and the desert shall rejoice and blossom as the rose. . . . —Isaiah 35:1 (NKJV)

25
TUESDAY

The heavens declare the glory of God; and the firmament shows His handiwork.
—Psalm 19:1 (NKJV)

WILFRED FUNK, the vocabulary expert and author, once listed what he considered the ten most beautiful words in the English language: *hush, mist, murmuring, dawn, tranquil, chimes, melody, golden, luminous,* and *lullaby.*

Not bad, I THOUGHT, *but he forgot* mercy *and* grace *and* generosity *and, the most beautiful of all,* love. Add love to any equation and you can transform it into a thing of beauty, even things we consider "unbeautiful."

For instance, not long ago I visited the zoo and watched a mother rhinoceros tenderly licking her new baby. "That's the ugliest baby I've ever seen. He's gross," said a young girl nearby.

And in truth he was fat and wrinkled, and his bulbous head was oversized for his body. But then I looked again at the loving attention junior was getting from his mother. He was beautiful in her eyes, and I decided

26
WEDNESDAY

So we have known and believe the love that God has for us. God is love, and those who abide in love abide in God, and God abides in them. —1 John 4:16 (NRSV)

27
THURSDAY

" . . . Shew I unto you a more excellent way." —1 Corinthians 12:31 (KJV)

28
FRIDAY

"My stronghold and my refuge, my savior; you save me from violence."
—2 Samuel 22:3 (ESV)

29
SATURDAY

Lo, I am with you always, even unto the end of the world. Amen.
—Matthew 28:20 (KJV)

Mama was right. Baby wasn't fat, just pleasingly plump. His mama's love had won me over.

Love: IT IS A beautiful *word*, and a beautiful deed too.

—*Fred Bauer*

PRAYER REQUESTS _____

_____

_____

_____

OCTOBER

S	M	T	W	T	F	S
						1
2	3	4	5	6	7	8
9	10	11	12	13	14	15
16	17	18	19	20	21	22
23/30	24/31	25	26	27	28	29

Thou shalt love the Lord thy God with all thy heart, and with all thy soul, and with all thy mind. —MATTHEW 22:37 (KJV)

A PRAYER FOR NOVEMBER

O come, let us unto the Lord
shout loud with singing voice.
to the rock of our saving health
let us make joyful noise.
Before his presence let us then
approach with thanksgiving:
also let us triumphantly
with Psalms unto him sing.

"PSALM 95," THE BAY PSALM BOOK (1640)

THE GREAT COMMANDMENT

I used to wonder why
You wanted me to love You, God,
And love You so completely.
It did seem strange to me,
For I knew You had
no human vanity
or need for reassurance,
And the love I had to offer
must have seemed so small,
just one more gift
among so many.

However,
As I've grown older
and wiser through experience,
I've come upon this one
illuminating truth:
By loving, we open ourselves
to being loved.

Now,
As I give my love to You
With all my heart and soul and mind,
I see You as You'd have me see You,
A God of awe and majesty
Who cannot be outgiven.
And so, my God, at last
I stand before You,
Heart defenseless,
Arms outstretched,
Waiting to receive the love You want
to squander on me!

☙ NOVEMBER 2016 ☙

SUNDAY	MONDAY	TUESDAY	WEDNESDAY	THURSDAY	FRIDAY	SATURDAY
		1 ALL SAINTS DAY	2 ALL SOULS DAY	3	4	5
6 DAYLIGHT SAVING TIME ENDS	7	8 ELECTION DAY	9	10	11 VETERANS DAY	12
13	14	15	16	17	18	19
20	21 GUIDEPOSTS THANKSGIVING DAY OF PRAYER	22	23	24 THANKSGIVING	25	26
27 1ST SUNDAY IN ADVENT	28	29	30			

NOTES

OCTOBER

S	M	T	W	T	F	S
						1
2	3	4	5	6	7	8
9	10	11	12	13	14	15
16	17	18	19	20	21	22
23/30	24/31	25	26	27	28	29

DECEMBER

S	M	T	W	T	F	S
				1	2	3
4	5	6	7	8	9	10
11	12	13	14	15	16	17
18	19	20	21	22	23	24
25	26	27	28	29	30	31

30
SUNDAY

But when you pray, go into your room, close the door and pray to your Father, who is unseen. Then your Father, who sees what is done in secret, will reward you. —Matthew 6:6 (NIV)

31
MONDAY

HALLOWEEN

"For my thoughts are not your thoughts, neither are your ways my ways," declares the Lord. —Isaiah 55:8 (NIV)

NOVEMBER

1
TUESDAY

ALL SAINTS DAY

Bear with each other and forgive one another if any of you has a grievance against someone. Forgive as the Lord forgave you. —Colossians 3:13 (NIV)

MY KIDS ARE ALWAYS SAYING I belong to the "peace-and-quiet" generation. Well, I guess they're right. Trouble is, I never seem to find enough of it. If the TV isn't blaring, the stereo is, or else there's a wrestling match on the family room floor, or the phone is ringing, or the dogs are barking, or there is a group of teenagers dancing in the basement or eating pizza in the kitchen. I learned, quite a few years ago, that if I was going to have any peace at all, I'd just have to find it on my own.

One thing that's helped me is to visualize a calm, crystal-clear lake within me and to let that symbolize the soothing Christ presence bathing me in His peace. I just hold that picture in mind until I really feel it wash over me and then come back to it again and again in the midst of the noise and confusion.

Oh, my nerves still get a bit jangled sometimes, but now I know that peace has more to

2
WEDNESDAY

ALL SOULS DAY

A good name is rather to be chosen than great riches. . . . —Proverbs 22:1 (KJV)

3
THURSDAY

And let us consider how we may spur one another on toward love and good deeds. —Hebrews 10:24 (NIV)

4
FRIDAY

"Go, sell everything you have and give to the poor. . . . " —Mark 10:21 (NIV)

5
SATURDAY

It is clear that the righteous one will live on the basis of faith. —Galatians 3:11 (CEB)

do with what's going on inside me than with what's going on around me.

If you belong to the peace-and-quiet generation but live in a whirling world, you might try this way of building your own inner chapel.

—*Marilyn Morgan King*

PRAYER REQUESTS _____

_____

_____

_____

NOVEMBER

S	M	T	W	T	F	S
		1	2	3	4	5
6	7	8	9	10	11	12
13	14	15	16	17	18	19
20	21	22	23	24	25	26
27	28	29	30			

6
SUNDAY

DAYLIGHT SAVINGS TIME ENDS

"There is so much more I want to tell you, but you can't understand it now."
—John 16:12 (TLB)

7
MONDAY

"Blessed are those who mourn, for they will be comforted." —Matthew 5:4 (NIV)

8
TUESDAY

ELECTION DAY

There is neither Jew nor Gentile, neither slave nor free, nor is there male and female, for you are all one in Christ Jesus. —Galatians 3:28 (NIV)

MY GRANDFATHER, a steam locomotive engineer, was my boyhood hero. On my seventeenth birthday, he invited me to ride in the cab on his night fast passenger run. Watching the telegraph poles blur by, I was thrilled at the speed of the roaring train. At our first stop, he climbed down to oil. I followed.

"Grandpa," I asked, "how come you're a nervous wreck in your car, but in your engine, going much faster, you're so calm?"

He pointed down the shining rails in the headlight's gleam. "See that mainline, Sonny? It was laid down, ballasted, secured, and is maintained by experts who know it has to keep heavy speeding trains like ours on the track. Even the switches to sidetracks and spurs are preset before we get to 'em to keep us going where we should go. Now in my automobile, I'm on my own. But up in my cab on the mainline, I know for sure some-

9
WEDNESDAY

Remember your word to your servant, for you have given me hope. —Psalm 119:49 (NIV)

10
THURSDAY

"Oh, that I could write my plea with an iron pen in the rock forever." —Job 19:23–24 (TLB)

11
FRIDAY

VETERANS
DAY

For, "Everyone who calls on the name of the Lord shall be saved." —Romans 10:13 (NRSV)

12
SATURDAY

"Let it be given them day by day without fail." —Ezra 6:9 (JPS)

one's always on the job looking out for us. Understand?"

I didn't then. But later I realized what a modern parable my beloved grandpa had given me.

—*Charles M. Davis*

PRAYER REQUESTS _____

_____

_____

_____

NOVEMBER

S	M	T	W	T	F	S
		1	2	3	4	5
6	7	8	9	10	11	12
13	14	15	16	17	18	19
20	21	22	23	24	25	26
27	28	29	30			

Good Father, Provider of everything I need,
help me to find rest and comfort in You.

13
SUNDAY

Jesus went down to Nazareth with them and was obedient to them. His mother cherished every word in her heart. —Luke 2:51 (CEB)

14
MONDAY

My son, do not forget my teaching, but let your heart keep my commandments, for lengths of days and years of life and peace they will add to you. —Proverbs 3:1–2 (ESV)

15
TUESDAY

When you pass through the waters, I will be with you; and when you pass through the rivers, they will not sweep over you. When you walk through the fire, you will not be burned; the flames will not set you ablaze. —Isaiah 43:2 (NIV)

VISITING FAMILY IN western New York, I anticipated a big dinner at my sister's. Because Mother was frail, I agreed to bake the ham and devil two dozen eggs on her behalf, in her kitchen.

But it was a bad cooking day. The eggs took ninety minutes to shell; the whites were so gouged, I should have made egg salad. And the ham? The outer half-inch of the shank was charred black. As for the pan juices, I figured we'd have to throw away the roaster.

If I'd been in my kitchen, I might have thrown it all away. But this wasn't my house. "We'll make do," Mom said, repeating a phrase that had gotten her and Dad through the Depression and the war rationing and us seven kids through college wearing hand-me-downs.

At my sister's, the family gathered in, four generations around the table. I sat next to five-year-old Kurtis. Despite my second-rate eggs and ham, the table was generously laden. Kurtis was the first to spoon up mashed potatoes. He nudged me. "Pass the gravy. Please."

I brought the meat. Never even thought of gravy. Child, are you kidding? Gravy? All this quickly went

16
WEDNESDAY

Love is patient; love is kind. . . . —1 Corinthians 13:4 (NRSV)

17
THURSDAY

So the Lord said to Joshua: "Get up! Why do you lie thus on your face?"
—Joshua 7:10 (NKJV)

18
FRIDAY

God will speak to this people, to whom he said, "This is the resting place, let the weary rest". . . . —Isaiah 28:11–12 (NIV)

19
SATURDAY

A man's gift maketh room for him, and bringeth him before great men.
—Proverbs 18:16 (KJV)

through my head, but I had the good sense to smile and model Mother's "make-do" way.

"There's no gravy," I said. "Today is a butter day."

I handed Kurtis the butter plate. He cut off a slab and shrugged as if to say, *Okay, butter will do.* And it did. We made do.

—*Evelyn Bence*

PRAYER REQUESTS _____

_____

_____

_____

NOVEMBER

S	M	T	W	T	F	S
		1	2	3	4	5
6	7	8	9	10	11	12
13	14	15	16	17	18	19
20	21	22	23	24	25	26
27	28	29	30			

OUR PRAYER

Thank You, Lord, for piles of laundry; my family has plenty of clothes to wear. Thank You for the sink of dirty dishes; everyone ate to their hearts' content. Thank You for bills; each represents a service I received. Thank You for my job; it provides for my loved ones.

20
SUNDAY

Hope does not disappoint. . . . —Romans 5:5 (NAS)

21
MONDAY

GUIDEPOSTS
THANKSGIVING
DAY OF PRAYER

Trust in the Lord with all thine heart; and lean not unto thine own understanding. —Proverbs 3:5 (KJV)

22
TUESDAY

You hem me in behind and before, and you lay your hand upon me. —Psalm 139:5 (NIV)

I DON'T HANDLE frustration and disappointment well. When something comes between me and my goal, I become almost frantic looking for an alternative. If a bad cold threatens to cancel a vacation, I start packing anyway. If a snowstorm means I can't drive to the library to look up the information I need for a report, I look for other ways to get there. So I was interested to hear what a professional quarterback had to say in an interview about a month after a season-ending injury.

When he was asked how he was dealing with the disappointment of being unable to finish the football season, he said: "Very badly, at first. But then I realized that God might be telling me to spend more time in some other areas of my life. I'm happy. I feel peaceful. I'm discovering that God was right. I needed to be with my family and my friends."

Now I follow his example whenever something disrupts my routine or comes between me and my goal. Instead of asking God to help me find a way

23
WEDNESDAY

Thus Samuel grew and the Lord was with him and let none of his words fail.
—1 Samuel 3:19 (NAS)

24
THURSDAY

THANKSGIVING

Oh, give thanks to the Lord, for He is good! For His mercy endures forever.
—Psalm 107:1 (NKJV)

25
FRIDAY

She watches over the affairs of her household and does not eat the bread of idleness. Her children arise and call her blessed. . . . —Proverbs 31:27–28 (NIV)

26
SATURDAY

"The Lord is my strength and song. . . ." —Exodus 15:2 (NAS)

to do something very important to me, I ask God to show me where I ought to use my energies. Not only has He led me in some surprising directions, but I also haven't encountered frustrations or disappointments along the way.

—Phyllis Hobe

PRAYER REQUESTS _____

_____

_____

_____

NOVEMBER

S	M	T	W	T	F	S
		1	2	3	4	5
6	7	8	9	10	11	12
13	14	15	16	17	18	19
20	21	22	23	24	25	26
27	28	29	30			

God, thank You for the tangible message that You,
the bright God of the heavens, are with me today and always.

27
SUNDAY

**1ST SUNDAY
IN ADVENT**

"But you, Bethlehem Ephrathah, though you are little among the thousands of Judah, yet out of you shall come forth to Me the One to be Ruler in Israel, whose goings forth are from of old, from everlasting." —Micah 5:2 (NKJV)

28
MONDAY

"And why worry about a speck in your friend's eye when you have a log in your own?" —Matthew 7:3 (NLT)

29
TUESDAY

Thy words have upholden him that was falling, and thou hast strengthened the feeble knees. —Job 4:4 (KJV)

WHEN ALICE IN WONDERLAND came to a fork in the road, she asked the Cheshire Cat, "Which road do I take?"

"Where do you want to go?" asked the Cheshire cat.

"I don't know," said Alice.

"Then it doesn't matter," replied the cat.

Every day, in some way, we face a fork in the road that does matter. Shall we yield to a good impulse? Resist a bad one? Shall we pass along that juicy bit of gossip or shall we keep it to ourselves?

30
WEDNESDAY

Children are a gift from the Lord; they are a reward from him. —Psalm 127:3 (NLT)

DECEMBER

1
THURSDAY

Spend your time and energy in the exercise of keeping spiritually fit. —1 Timothy 4:7 (TLB)

2
FRIDAY

And the shepherds returned, glorifying and praising God for all the things that they had heard and seen. . . . —Luke 2:20 (KJV)

3
SATURDAY

Before a word is on my tongue you, Lord, know it completely. —Psalm 139:4 (NIV)

When I face a fork in the road each day, I ask God to help me choose the right way. I think it determines whether I grow spiritually or shrink.

—*Sidney Fields*

PRAYER REQUESTS _____

_____

_____

_____

NOVEMBER

S	M	T	W	T	F	S
		1	2	3	4	5
6	7	8	9	10	11	12
13	14	15	16	17	18	19
20	21	22	23	24	25	26
27	28	29	30			

Thou shalt love thy neighbour as thyself. —MATTHEW 22:39 (KJV)

A PRAYER FOR DECEMBER

Ah, dearest Jesus, Holy Child,
Make Thee a bed, soft, undefiled,
Within my heart, that it may be
A quiet chamber kept for Thee.

MARTIN LUTHER (1483–1546)

AND THE SECOND IS LIKE UNTO IT...

Dear Jesus,
Why all this fuss about neighbors?
Neighborhoods have changed a lot,
You know.
People come and go,
And neighborhoods lack identity today.
Why, my last neighbor
Was here just three months,
And the ones who moved in today
Said they get transferred every year.
They aren't even American citizens...
Do you expect me to believe
That a coincidence of time and place
Bonds me to these neighbors?
You do, don't You?
Now that I think about it
The message I should get
From my new neighbors
Is that the world is getting smaller
And moving faster.
You didn't tell me to categorize
Neighbors, did You, God?
You said: "Love thy neighbor."
And loving these new and different neighbors
Is more important today
Than it has ever been,
Isn't it?
God, I'm going to love
These new neighbors of mine
Until they love me too.

❧ DECEMBER 2016 ❧

SUNDAY	MONDAY	TUESDAY	WEDNESDAY	THURSDAY	FRIDAY	SATURDAY
				1	2	3
4 2ND SUNDAY IN ADVENT	5	6	7	8	9	10
11 3RD SUNDAY IN ADVENT	12	13	14	15	16	17
18 4TH SUNDAY IN ADVENT	19	20	21 WINTER BEGINS	22	23	24 CHRISTMAS EVE
25 CHRISTMAS / HANUKKAH	26	27	28	29	30	31 NEW YEAR'S EVE

NOTES

NOVEMBER

S	M	T	W	T	F	S
		1	2	3	4	5
6	7	8	9	10	11	12
13	14	15	16	17	18	19
20	21	22	23	24	25	26
27	28	29	30			

JANUARY 2017

S	M	T	W	T	F	S
1	2	3	4	5	6	7
8	9	10	11	12	13	14
15	16	17	18	19	20	21
22	23	24	25	26	27	28
29	30	31				

Lord, thank You for the hope that comes from those who truly know You. Amen.

4
SUNDAY

2ND SUNDAY
IN ADVENT

"Behold, the days are coming, declares the Lord, when I will raise up for David a righteous Branch, and he shall reign as king and deal wisely, and shall execute justice and righteousness in the land." —Jeremiah 23:5 (ESV)

5
MONDAY

Train up a child in the way he should go, and when he is old he will not depart from it. —Proverbs 22:6 (NKJV)

6
TUESDAY

They prayed for the new believers there that they might receive the Holy Spirit. —Acts 8:15 (NIV)

WHEN WORK NEEDED SOMEONE to dress up as a bear for story time, guess who volunteered? Yes, anything to distract me from the phone call I knew I had to make to apologize to a friend.

While I struggled to don the heavy costume, the long paws and the hairy hands with four-inch nails, I had visions of how happy the children would be to see me. But as I lumbered through the store, only two or three kids appeared that way. The others scattered in terror.

Since bears aren't supposed to speak, I could only watch silently and couldn't say what I wanted to: "I came to make you happy. I won't hurt. Come up to me, please." But even if I could have given voice to my words, they wouldn't have been heard over the shrieks and tears.

Inside my costume, I had to laugh. Wasn't I that way too many times with God? A difficult phone call to mend a friendship, my fear of driving—maybe God was handing me those challenges as loving

7
WEDNESDAY

"Isn't this the carpenter's son? . . . " —Matthew 13:55 (NIV)

8
THURSDAY

Whoever walks with the wise becomes wise. . . . —Proverbs 13:20 (ESV)

9
FRIDAY

Fixing our eyes on Jesus, the pioneer and perfecter of faith. . . . —Hebrews 12:2 (NIV)

10
SATURDAY

"A Savior has been born to you; he is the Messiah, the Lord." —Luke 2:11 (NIV)

gifts, and there I was screaming, "No, go away!"

As I made my way to the back room, I knew that as soon as I yanked off my paws, I'd be dialing my friend's phone number to make that overdue apology.

—Linda Neukrug

PRAYER REQUESTS _____

_____

_____

_____

DECEMBER

S	M	T	W	T	F	S
				1	2	3
4	5	6	7	8	9	10
11	12	13	14	15	16	17
18	19	20	21	22	23	24
25	26	27	28	29	30	31

OUR PRAYER

Lord, You bless me everywhere,
even in places I think I don't want to be.

11
SUNDAY

3RD SUNDAY
IN ADVENT

Now there were in the same country shepherds living out in the fields, keeping watch over their flock by night. —Luke 2:8 (NKJV)

12
MONDAY

So then, brothers, stand firm and hold to the traditions that you were taught by us. . . . —2 Thessalonians 2:15 (ESV)

13
TUESDAY

Isn't it obvious that all the angels are sent to help out. . . ? —Hebrews 1:14 (MSG)

EVERY THURSDAY IS my wife's choir rehearsal. One night, Ruby and her friend Iza left for church. I waved good-bye and returned to my chores, when the doorbell rang. A friend stood with eyes cast downward. Something was wrong!

"Your wife's been in a head-on crash," he said.

"Is she all right?" I asked, trembling.

He paused, shook his head, and muttered, "I don't know." He drove me to the church. My heart raced, and my hands turned icy. The drive seemed endless.

A crowd was huddled outside, and there was no ambulance. Had they already been taken to the hospital? As we approached, the choir director stepped from the crowd, her face dark with worry. "Ruby and Iza are all right but shaken up," she said. "A car from across the street was left unattended with its motor running. It rolled from the curb, hitting Ruby's car head-on."

I thanked God as I drove Ruby and Iza to the hospital. Upon their release, though still unnerved, they both insisted on returning to choir rehearsal. Later, Ruby even drove home.

14
WEDNESDAY

But if we hope for what we do not yet have, we wait for it patiently. —Romans 8:25 (NIV)

15
THURSDAY

Do nothing out of selfish ambition or vain conceit. Rather, in humility value others above yourselves, not looking to your own interests but each of you to the interests of the others. —Philippians 2:3–4 (NIV)

16
FRIDAY

And seek the peace of the city whither I have caused you to be carried away captives . . . for in the peace thereof shall ye have peace. —Jeremiah 29:7 (KJV)

17
SATURDAY

Now to him who . . . is able to do far more abundantly than all that we ask or think, to him be glory. . . . —Ephesians 3:20–21 (RSV)

Ruby and Iza showed courage. But what impressed me most was their devotion to the choir and their consideration for others. These are the qualities one respects in others. These are the qualities that make me love my wife all the more.

—Oscar Greene

PRAYER REQUESTS _____

_____

_____

_____

DECEMBER

S	M	T	W	T	F	S
				1	2	3
4	5	6	7	8	9	10
11	12	13	14	15	16	17
18	19	20	21	22	23	24
25	26	27	28	29	30	31

Father, there is nowhere on earth I would rather be
than in the manger with You.

18
SUNDAY

4TH SUNDAY
IN ADVENT

And suddenly there was with the angel a multitude of the heavenly host praising God and saying: "Glory to God in the highest, and on earth peace, goodwill toward men!" —Luke 2:13–14 (NKJV)

19
MONDAY

What shall I take to witness for thee? . . . —Lamentations 2:13 (JPS)

20
TUESDAY

Your Father knows what you need before you ask him. —Matthew 6:8 (NIV)

WINTER. SOME DO NOT LIKE it much but endure it. But some of us are devoted lovers of it. While, now and then, we grumble at the ice and snow, we really don't mind winter all that much. And, believe it or not, we like it most of the time.

Returning from an afternoon walk on Quaker's Hill, where we live, my wife and I stopped, arrested by the beauty of the scene before us. Our house, atop a hill, stood etched in white against a blue sky, its stately columns gleaming in the early setting of the sun. Snow lay deep upon the ground, festooned on bushes and trees. The long white fences ran off into the distance, lined by gigantic maples, stark and black against the white-clad hills. Long shafts of golden sunlight lay across the snow-covered lawns as evening came down cold and stern.

Winter silences have their meaningful appeal to the reflective mind. Gliding cross-country on skis into a lonely grove of trees, then standing still

21
WEDNESDAY

WINTER BEGINS

God is our . . . source of all comfort. —2 Corinthians 1:3 (NLT)

22
THURSDAY

In Your light we see light. —Psalm 36:9 (NAS)

23
FRIDAY

They came . . . and found. . . . —Luke 2:16 (KJV)

24
SATURDAY

CHRISTMAS EVE

[Jesus Christ] was chosen before the creation of the world, but was revealed in these last times for your sake. —1 Peter 1:20 (NIV)

and quiet until the palpable silence makes itself felt, is to be at one with the essence of life. And so it is that in winter, nature's utter and incredible stillness steals upon one, and the healing of her gentle touch is felt.

—*Norman Vincent Peale*

PRAYER REQUESTS _____

_____

_____

_____

DECEMBER

S	M	T	W	T	F	S
				1	2	3
4	5	6	7	8	9	10
11	12	13	14	15	16	17
18	19	20	21	22	23	24
25	26	27	28	29	30	31

25
SUNDAY

CHRISTMAS /
HANUKKAH

Therefore the Lord Himself will give you a sign: Behold, the virgin shall conceive and bear a Son, and shall call His name Immanuel. —Isaiah 7:14 (NKJV)

26
MONDAY

You have let me experience the joys of life and the exquisite pleasures of your own eternal presence. —Psalm 16:11 (TLB)

27
TUESDAY

"He changes the seasons and guides history. . . ." —Daniel 2:21 (MSG)

MARTHA DEAN, a former TV interviewer, began telling me about interesting women who'd been on her show. "One of the nicest was Myrna Loy. And she was so generous. She was wearing a beautiful sweater, which I admired, and she said, 'Take it! I've had all the pleasure I'm going to get out of this sweater and I want you to have it.'

"I didn't take it, naturally. But later I kind of wished I had. Our engineer told me I should have because she really wanted me to have that sweater. It would have given her so much joy."

What is it that makes us reluctant to accept gifts? Are we afraid of seeming selfish? Or do we feel undeserving? Often there is a fear of obligation: "Oh dear, now she will expect something from me." Yet the true giver wants us to have what is freely offered. The true giver is not sitting in judgment, finding us weak and unworthy. By the very gift, she is saying, "I think you're great." Nor does the true giver ask or expect anything in return. Her reward is in the sheer joy of giving.

28
WEDNESDAY

Pray without ceasing. —1 Thessalonians 5:17 (NAS)

29
THURSDAY

My sheep hear my voice. I know them, and they follow me. —John 10:27 (NRSV)

30
FRIDAY

Forgive others, and God will forgive you. —Luke 6:37 (CEV)

31
SATURDAY

NEW YEAR'S EVE

It is God's privilege to conceal things. . . . —Proverbs 25:2 (TLB)

This is true of genuinely nice people. And it is true of God, Who gave us the gift of life. He wants us to have that life in all its abundance. Jesus Himself said that was one of the reasons He came. We, then, should hold out grateful hands to accept.

—*Marjorie Holmes*

PRAYER REQUESTS _____

_____

_____

_____

DECEMBER

S	M	T	W	T	F	S
				1	2	3
4	5	6	7	8	9	10
11	12	13	14	15	16	17
18	19	20	21	22	23	24
25	26	27	28	29	30	31

JANUARY 2017

SUNDAY	MONDAY	TUESDAY	WEDNESDAY	THURSDAY	FRIDAY	SATURDAY
1 NEW YEAR'S DAY	2	3	4	5	6	7
8	9	10	11	12	13	14
15	16 MARTIN LUTHER KING JR. DAY	17	18	19	20	21
22	23	24	25	26	27	28
29	30	31				

FEBRUARY 2017

SUNDAY	MONDAY	TUESDAY	WEDNESDAY	THURSDAY	FRIDAY	SATURDAY
		1	2	3	4	
5	6	7	8	9	10	11
12 ABRAHAM LINCOLN'S BIRTHDAY	13	14 VALENTINE'S DAY	15	16	17	18
19	20 PRESIDENTS' DAY	21	22 GEORGE WASHINGTON'S BIRTHDAY	23	24	25
26	27	28				

MARCH 2017

SUNDAY	MONDAY	TUESDAY	WEDNES-	THURSDAY	FRIDAY	SATURDAY
			1 ASH WEDNESDAY	2	3	4
5	6	7	8	9	10	11
12 DAYLIGHT SAVING TIME BEGINS	13	14	15	16	17 ST. PATRICK'S DAY	18
19	20 SPRING BEGINS	21	22	23	24	25
26	27	28	29	30	31	

APRIL 2017

SUNDAY	MONDAY	TUESDAY	WEDNES-	THURSDAY	FRIDAY	SATURDAY
						1
2	3	4	5	6	7	8
9 PALM SUNDAY	10	11 PASSOVER	12	13 MAUNDY THURSDAY	14 GUIDEPOSTS GOOD FRIDAY DAY OF PRAYER	15
16 EASTER	17	18	19	20	21	22 EARTH DAY
23 30	24	25	26	27	28	29

2017 CALENDAR

JANUARY
S	M	T	W	T	F	S
1	2	3	4	5	6	7
8	9	10	11	12	13	14
15	16	17	18	19	20	21
22	23	24	25	26	27	28
29	30	31				

FEBRUARY
S	M	T	W	T	F	S
			1	2	3	4
5	6	7	8	9	10	11
12	13	14	15	16	17	18
19	20	21	22	23	24	25
26	27	28				

MARCH
S	M	T	W	T	F	S
			1	2	3	4
5	6	7	8	9	10	11
12	13	14	15	16	17	18
19	20	21	22	23	24	25
26	27	28	29	30	31	

APRIL
S	M	T	W	T	F	S
						1
2	3	4	5	6	7	8
9	10	11	12	13	14	15
16	17	18	19	20	21	22
23/30	24	25	26	27	28	29

MAY
S	M	T	W	T	F	S
	1	2	3	4	5	6
7	8	9	10	11	12	13
14	15	16	17	18	19	20
21	22	23	24	25	26	27
28	29	30	31			

JUNE
S	M	T	W	T	F	S
				1	2	3
4	5	6	7	8	9	10
11	12	13	14	15	16	17
18	19	20	21	22	23	24
25	26	27	28	29	30	

JULY
S	M	T	W	T	F	S
						1
2	3	4	5	6	7	8
9	10	11	12	13	14	15
16	17	18	19	20	21	22
23/30	24/31	25	26	27	28	29

AUGUST
S	M	T	W	T	F	S
		1	2	3	4	5
6	7	8	9	10	11	12
13	14	15	16	17	18	19
20	21	22	23	24	25	26
27	28	29	30	31		

SEPTEMBER
S	M	T	W	T	F	S
					1	2
3	4	5	6	7	8	9
10	11	12	13	14	15	16
17	18	19	20	21	22	23
24	25	26	27	28	29	30

OCTOBER
S	M	T	W	T	F	S
1	2	3	4	5	6	7
8	9	10	11	12	13	14
15	16	17	18	19	20	21
22	23	24	25	26	27	28
29	30	31				

NOVEMBER
S	M	T	W	T	F	S
			1	2	3	4
5	6	7	8	9	10	11
12	13	14	15	16	17	18
19	20	21	22	23	24	25
26	27	28	29	30		

DECEMBER
S	M	T	W	T	F	S
					1	2
3	4	5	6	7	8	9
10	11	12	13	14	15	16
17	18	19	20	21	22	23
24/31	25	26	27	28	29	30

2018 CALENDAR

JANUARY
S	M	T	W	T	F	S
	1	2	3	4	5	6
7	8	9	10	11	12	13
14	15	16	17	18	19	20
21	22	23	24	25	26	27
28	29	30	31			

FEBRUARY
S	M	T	W	T	F	S
				1	2	3
4	5	6	7	8	9	10
11	12	13	14	15	16	17
18	19	20	21	22	23	24
25	26	27	28			

MARCH
S	M	T	W	T	F	S
				1	2	3
4	5	6	7	8	9	10
11	12	13	14	15	16	17
18	19	20	21	22	23	24
25	26	27	28	29	30	31

APRIL
S	M	T	W	T	F	S
1	2	3	4	5	6	7
8	9	10	11	12	13	14
15	16	17	18	19	20	21
22	23	24	25	26	27	28
29	30					

MAY
S	M	T	W	T	F	S
		1	2	3	4	5
6	7	8	9	10	11	12
13	14	15	16	17	18	19
20	21	22	23	24	25	26
27	28	29	30	31		

JUNE
S	M	T	W	T	F	S
					1	2
3	4	5	6	7	8	9
10	11	12	13	14	15	16
17	18	19	20	21	22	23
24	25	26	27	28	29	30

JULY
S	M	T	W	T	F	S
1	2	3	4	5	6	7
8	9	10	11	12	13	14
15	16	17	18	19	20	21
22	23	24	25	26	27	28
29	30	31				

AUGUST
S	M	T	W	T	F	S
			1	2	3	4
5	6	7	8	9	10	11
12	13	14	15	16	17	18
19	20	21	22	23	24	25
26	27	28	29	30	31	

SEPTEMBER
S	M	T	W	T	F	S
						1
2	3	4	5	6	7	8
9	10	11	12	13	14	15
16	17	18	19	20	21	22
23/30	24	25	26	27	28	29

OCTOBER
S	M	T	W	T	F	S
	1	2	3	4	5	6
7	8	9	10	11	12	13
14	15	16	17	18	19	20
21	22	23	24	25	26	27
28	29	30	31			

NOVEMBER
S	M	T	W	T	F	S
				1	2	3
4	5	6	7	8	9	10
11	12	13	14	15	16	17
18	19	20	21	22	23	24
25	26	27	28	29	30	

DECEMBER
S	M	T	W	T	F	S
						1
2	3	4	5	6	7	8
9	10	11	12	13	14	15
16	17	18	19	20	21	22
23/30	24/31	25	26	27	28	29

❧ HOLIDAYS ❧

HOLIDAY	2017	2018	2019
New Year's Day	Sunday, January 1	Monday, January 1	Tuesday, January 1
Martin Luther King Jr. Day	Monday, January 16	Monday, January 15	Monday, January 21
Abraham Lincoln's Birthday	Sunday, February 12	Monday, February 12	Tuesday, February 12
Valentine's Day	Tuesday, February 14	Wednesday, February 14	Thursday, February 14
Presidents' Day	Monday, February 20	Monday, February 19	Monday, February 18
Ash Wednesday	Wednesday, March 1	Wednesday, February 14	Wednesday, March 6
George Washington's Birthday	Wednesday, February 22	Thursday, February 22	Friday, February 22
St. Patrick's Day	Friday, March 17	Saturday, March 17	Sunday, March 17
Palm Sunday	Sunday, April 9	Sunday, March 25	Sunday, April 14
Passover	Tuesday, April 11	Saturday, March 31	Saturday, April 20
Good Friday	Friday, April 14	Friday, March 30	Friday, April 19
Easter	Sunday, April 16	Sunday, April 1	Sunday, April 21
Earth Day	Saturday, April 22	Sunday, April 22	Monday, April 22
Mother's Day	Sunday, May 14	Sunday, May 13	Sunday, May 12
Pentecost	Sunday, June 4	Sunday, May 20	Sunday, June 9
Memorial Day	Monday, May 29	Monday, May 28	Monday, May 27
Flag Day	Wednesday, June 14	Thursday, June 14	Friday, June 14
Father's Day	Sunday, June 18	Sunday, June 17	Sunday, June 16
Independence Day	Tuesday, July 4	Wednesday, July 4	Thursday, July 4
Labor Day	Monday, September 4	Monday, September 3	Monday, September 2
Rosh Hashanah	Thursday, September 21	Monday, September 10	Monday, September 30
Yom Kippur	Saturday, September 30	Wednesday, September 19	Wednesday, October 9
United Nations Day	Tuesday, October 24	Wednesday, October 24	Thursday, October 24
Halloween	Tuesday, October 31	Wednesday, October 31	Thursday, October 31
Election Day	Tuesday, November 7	Tuesday, November 6	Tuesday, November 5
Veterans Day	Saturday, November 11	Sunday, November 11	Monday, November 11
Thanksgiving	Thursday, November 23	Thursday, November 22	Thursday, November 28
Hanukkah	Wednesday, December 13	Monday, December 3	Monday, December 23
Christmas Eve	Sunday, December 24	Monday, December 24	Tuesday, December 24
Christmas	Monday, December 25	Tuesday, December 25	Wednesday, December 25
New Year's Eve	Sunday, December 31	Monday, December 31	Tuesday, December 31

❧ BIRTHDAYS ❧

JANUARY

_____
_____
_____
_____
_____
_____
_____
_____
_____
_____
_____

FEBRUARY

_____
_____
_____
_____
_____
_____
_____
_____
_____
_____
_____

MARCH

_____
_____
_____
_____
_____
_____
_____
_____
_____
_____
_____

APRIL

_____
_____
_____
_____
_____
_____
_____
_____
_____
_____
_____

MAY

_____
_____
_____
_____
_____
_____
_____
_____
_____
_____
_____

JUNE

_____
_____
_____
_____
_____
_____
_____
_____
_____
_____
_____

JULY

AUGUST

SEPTEMBER

OCTOBER

NOVEMBER

DECEMBER

❧ NAMES & NUMBERS ❧

NAME	ADDRESS	TELEPHONE

NAME   ADDRESS   TELEPHONE

❧ PRAYER REQUESTS ❧

❧ A NOTE FROM THE EDITORS ❧

Guideposts Daily Planner is created each year by the Books and Inspirational Media Division of Guideposts, a nonprofit organization that touches millions of lives every day through products and services that inspire, encourage, help you grow in your faith, and celebrate God's love.

Your purchase of *Guideposts Daily Planner 2016* makes a difference. When you buy Guideposts products, you're helping fund our many outreach programs to military personnel, prisons, hospitals, nursing homes, and educational institutions. If you'd like to be part of Guideposts' ministries by making a contribution, please visit GuidepostsFoundation.org to find out more about ways you can help.

You can order the 2017 edition of *Guideposts Daily Planner* anytime after July 2016. To order, visit ShopGuideposts.org, call (800) 932-2145, or write Guideposts, PO Box 5815, Harlan, Iowa 51593.

Guideposts Daily Planner 2016

ISBN-10: 0-8249-0452-4
ISBN-13: 978-0-8249-0452-4

Published by Guideposts Books & Inspirational Media
110 William Street
New York, New York 10038
Guideposts.org

Distributed by Ideals Publications, a Guideposts company
2630 Elm Hill Pike, Suite 100
Nashville, TN 37214

Guideposts, *Ideals*, and *Guideposts Daily Planner* are registered trademarks of Guideposts.

Acknowledgments

Every attempt has been made to credit the sources of copyrighted material used in this book. If any such acknowledgment has been inadvertently omitted or miscredited, receipt of such information would be appreciated.

Scripture quotations marked (ASV) are taken from *American Standard Version of the Bible*.

Scripture quotations marked (CEB) are taken from the *Common English Bible*. Copyright © 2011 by Common English Bible.

Scripture quotations marked (CEV) are taken from *Holy Bible: Contemporary English Version*. Copyright © 1995 American Bible Society.

Scripture quotations marked (ESV) are taken from the *Holy Bible, English Standard Version*, copyright © 2001 by Crossway Bibles, a division of Good News Publishers. Used by permission. All rights reserved.

Scripture quotations marked (GNT) are taken from the *Good News Translation*. Copyright © 1992 by American Bible Society.

Scripture quotations marked (HCS) are taken from *Holman Christian Standard Bible*. Copyright © 1999, 2000, 2002, 2003, 2009 by Holman Bible Publishers, Nashville Tennessee. All rights reserved.

Scripture quotations marked (JPS) are taken from the 1917 or 1985 edition of *Tanakh: A New Translation of the Holy Scriptures according to the Traditional Hebrew Text*. Copyright © 1985 by the Jewish Publication Society. All rights reserved.

Scripture quotations marked (KJV) are taken from *The King James Version of the Bible*.

Scripture quotations marked (MSG) are taken from *The Message*. Copyright © 1993, 1994, 1995, 1996, 2000, 2001, 2002 by Eugene H. Peterson.

Scripture quotations marked (NAS) are taken from the *New American Standard Bible*, copyright © 1960, 1962, 1963, 1968, 1971, 1972, 1973, 1975, 1977, 1995 by the Lockman Foundation. Used by permission.

Scripture quotations marked (NET) are taken from *New English Translation Bible*. Copyright © 1996–2006 by Biblical Studies Press, LLC. http://netbible.com. All rights reserved.

Scripture quotations marked (NIRV) are taken from the *New International Reader's Version*. Copyright © 1996, 1998 by Biblica.

Scripture quotations marked (NIV) are taken from *The Holy Bible, New International Version*. Copyright © 1973, 1978, 1984, 2011 by Biblica.

Scripture quotations marked (NKJV) are taken from *The Holy Bible, New King James Version*. Copyright © 1997, 1990, 1985, 1983 by Thomas Nelson, Inc.

Scripture quotations marked (NLT) are from the *Holy Bible, New Living Translation*. Copyright© 1996, 2004, 2007 by Tyndale House Foundation. Used by permission of Tyndale House Publishers Inc., Carol Stream, Illinois 60188. All rights reserved.

Scripture quotations marked (NRSV) are taken from the *New Revised Standard Version Bible*. Copyright © 1989 by the Division of Christian Education of the National Council of the Churches of Christ in the United States of America. Used by permission. All rights reserved.

Scripture quotations marked (RSV) are taken from the *Revised Standard Version of the Bible*. Copyright © 1946, 1952, 1971 by Division of Christian Education of the National Council of Churches of Christ in the United States of America. Used by permission.

Scripture quotations marked (TIB) are taken from *The Inclusive Bible: The First Egalitarian Translation*. Copyright © 2007 by Priests for Equality. All rights reserved.

Scripture quotations marked (TLB) are taken from *The Living Bible*. Copyright © 1971 by Tyndale House Publishers, Wheaton, Illinois 60187. All rights reserved.

Cover & interior design and typesetting by Müllerhaus
Cover photo by Shutterstock

Printed and bound in the United States of America
10 9 8 7 6 5 4 3 2 1